Practical social work

Published in conjunction with
the British Association of Social Workers
Series Editor: Jo Campling

BASW

Social work is at an important stage in its development. The profession is facing fresh challenges to work flexibly in fast-changing social and organisational environments. New requirements for training are also demanding a more critical and reflective, as well as more highly skilled, approach to practice.

The British Association of Social Workers has always been conscious of its role in setting guidelines for practice and in seeking to raise professional standards. The concept of the *Practical Social Work* series was conceived to fulfil a genuine professional need for a carefully planned, coherent series of texts that would stimulate and inform debate, thereby contributing to the development of practitioners' skills and professionalism.

Newly relaunched, the series continues to address the needs of all those who are looking to deepen and refresh their understanding and skills. It is designed for students and busy professionals alike. Each book marries practice issues and challenges with the latest theory and research in a compact and applied format. The authors represent a wide variety of experience both as educators and practitioners. Taken together, the books set a standard in their clarity, relevance and rigour.

A list of new and best-selling titles in this series follows overleaf. A comprehensive list of titles available in the series, and further details about individual books, can be found online at :
www.palgrave.com/socialworkpolicy/basw

Series standing order **ISBN 0–333–80313–2**

You can receive future titles in this series as they are published by placing a standing order. Please contact your bookseller or, in the case of difficulty, contact us at the address below with your name and address, the title of the series and the ISBN quoted above.

Customer Services Department, Macmillan Distribution Ltd, Houndmills, Basingstoke, Hampshire RG21 6XS, England

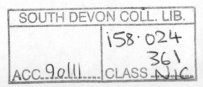

Practical social work series

New and best-selling titles

Robert Adams *Social Work and Empowerment* *(3rd edition)*

Sarah Banks *Ethics and Values in Social Work (3rd edition)* **new!**

James G. Barber *Social Work with Addictions (2nd edition)*

Suzy Braye and Michael Preston-Shoot *Practising Social Work Law (2nd edition)*

Veronica Coulshed and Joan Orme *Social Work Practice (4th edition)* **new!**

Veronica Coulshed and Audrey Mullender with David N. Jones and Neil Thompson
Management in Social Work (3rd edition) **new!**

Lena Dominelli *Anti-Racist Social Work (2nd edition)*

Celia Doyle *Working with Abused Children (3rd edition)* **new!**

Tony Jeffs and Mark Smith (editors) *Youth Work*

Joyce Lishman *Communication in Social Work*

Paula Nicolson and Rowan Bayne and Jenny Owen *Applied Psychology for Social
Workers (3rd edition)* **new!**

Judith Phillips, Mo Ray and Mary Marshall *Social Work with Older People
(4th edition)* **new!**

Michael Oliver and Bob Sapey *Social Work with Disabled People (3rd edition)* **new!**

Michael Preston-Shoot *Effective Groupwork*

Steven Shardlow and Mark Doel *Practice Learning and Teaching*

Neil Thompson *Anti-Discriminatory Practice (4th edition)* **new!**

Derek Tilbury *Working with Mental Illness (2nd edition)*

Alan Twelvetrees *Community Work (3rd edition)*

paula nicolson, rowan bayne
and jenny owen

applied psychology
for social workers

third edition

palgrave
macmillan

First edition 1984
Second edition 1990
Third edition 2006

Published by
PALGRAVE MACMILLAN
Houndmills, Basingstoke, Hampshire RG21 6XS and
175 Fifth Avenue, New York, N.Y. 10010
Companies and representatives throughout the world

PALGRAVE MACMILLAN is the global academic imprint of the Palgrave Macmillan division of St. Martin's Press, LLC and of Palgrave Macmillan Ltd.
Macmillan is a registered trademark in the United States, United Kingdom and other countries. Palgrave is a registered trademark in the European Union and other countries.

ISBN-13: 978–1–4039–4566–2
ISBN-10: 1–4039–4566–7

This book is printed on paper suitable for recycling and made from fully managed and sustained forest sources.

A catalogue record for this book is available from the British Library.

A catalog record for this book is available from the Library of Congress.

Library of Congress Catalog Card Number: 2005057480

10   9   8   7   6   5   4   3   2
15   14   13   12   11   10   09   08   07   06

Printed in China

Contents

List of tables

| Acknowledgements

Paula Nicolson has been greatly encouraged by the support of Jo Campling and the publishing team at Palgrave Macmillan, who have all helped to make the book so successful over the twenty and more years since it was originally published. She would also like to thank her colleagues, at the University of Sheffield and beyond, for providing academic inspiration from a range of interdisciplinary perspectives, and of course Derry and Kate Nicolson (and more recently Malachi, Azriel and Darren) for ongoing support.

Rowan Bayne would like to thank the many people who introduced him to the different aspects of interviewing and counselling, especially Clive Fletcher, Alec Rodger, Edgar Anstey and Chris Lewis (selection interviewing) and Francesca Inskipp, Peter Cook, Ian Horton and Tony Merry (counselling). A very warm 'thank you' to them and to Tracy Boakes for word-processing skilfully, quickly and positively.

Jenny Owen would like to thank colleagues at the University of Sheffield who have talked over ideas related to the themes of this book, and have raised useful questions – particularly Jo Cooke, Hilary Smith and Graham Smith. And thanks to Richard Jenkins, Jack Owen and Ruth Owen for tea and (always constructive) arguments.

Paula Nicolson, Rowan Bayne and Jenny Owen
Royal Holloway, University of London,
University of Sheffield and University of East London

This book is dedicated to the memory of my long-time friend and colleague **Precilla Y.L. Choi** who died suddenly in May 2005

Paula Nicolson

Introduction

Social work is about working with people to achieve change.
British Association of Social Workers, http://www.basw.co.uk

The first edition of *Applied Psychology for Social Workers* appeared more than twenty years ago in 1984. Since then there have been many changes both in social work organisation, training and delivery and in psychology as an academic and applied discipline. However, as highlighted by the extract above, the challenges underlying the practice of social work remain the same even if the context, process and structures are different. Social workers work with people. That means that a working knowledge of psychology is vital.

Psychology, therefore, continues to be a popular and essential component in the training of social workers, and even cursory examination of the social work curriculum and the outline of social work courses across the English-speaking world reinforces this observation. All social work courses continue to include, in some form, the theory and practice of human communication, understanding other people, personality, emotions and behaviour and the psychological elements of human systems such as work and care organisations and the family. The new social work curriculum in the UK gives greater priority than ever to the study and understanding of human growth and development. Psychology and social work theory and practice therefore remain intrinsically linked.

Why is there demand for a third edition of *Applied Psychology for Social Workers*?

The past thirty years have witnessed a constant cycle of changes in the training of social workers and expectations about their role and practice encouraged by political and economic pressures. Since the antisocial impulses were brought under control so that a process of internalisation through which children moved from external behavioural controls (rewards and punishments) to internal self-controls occurred. This transition linked with children's feelings towards their parents. Parental pressure towards socialisation makes children angry, and the thought of expressing this anger arouses their anxiety: partly because they might lose their parents if they were to express their anger too fervently. Children therefore repress their anger and turn it in on themselves. This is the foundation of 'guilt' – a powerful motivating force in development. The internalisation of the parents' (and thus society's) rules are embodied in the superego which is a harsh, punitive and inflexible psychological mechanism.

Behavioural psychology

Many social workers are now familiar with behaviour modification and more recently cognitive behaviour therapy (CBT) therapeutic techniques based upon knowledge derived from the behavioural school of psychology. This is one of the earliest approaches to understanding human behaviour developed initially by Thorndike, Watson, Pavlov and Skinner in the late 19th and early 20th centuries. Behaviourists are interested in questions relating to the conditions and events surrounding behaviour, that is, what actually happened before someone broke into tears, and what events took place in response to this. Psychologists from this perspective limit themselves to observable events, and the ways in which behaviour is influenced by the environment. This is directly opposed to the psychoanalytic approach which concentrates on the inner and unconscious life of individuals, and stresses the significance of biology in determining development. Behaviourism is concerned with how individuals learn about the way in which they can best exist within their environment, including emotional development, perceptions of the external world, social behaviour and personality. Individuals learn by making connections between events in the environment. Two particular theories have been developed to explain learning. These are classical conditioning and operant conditioning.

Studies of classical conditioning from the work of Pavlov who noticed that dogs salivated when they saw and smelled the food being brought to them. A bell sounded just before the time that the food arrived, and Pavlov observed that the dogs would eventually salivate on hearing the bell, even when there was no food to be seen or smelled. People learn to anticipate relationships between 'stimuli' in order to make sense of the world. A child might learn that when her father has had too much to drink he hits her, and the pain makes her cry. Thus, when she hears her father returning from the pub she responds by bursting into tears before he has a chance to be violent. She has learnt that the combination of her father returning home and the place that he has been indicate punishment for her. This is an example of classical conditioning.

Operant conditioning, based on the work of Skinner (1953), occurs when an individual learns that some behaviour of his/her own leads to a particular consequence. A boy may take part in a range of activities at home, but when he plays with guns, and behaves in a typically 'masculine' way, his mother smiles at him. He therefore learns to behave in this way more frequently, as it gains his mother's approval. This process has been studied by Skinner, who demon-strated that behaviour in rats and pigeons can be 'conditioned' if responses are followed by 'reinforcement' – the reward or punishment following particular manifestations of behaviour. The mother smiling at the little boy's games is the reinforcement. Conversely, a little girl playing with guns may have them taken from her, or be told with a frown that her behaviour is 'unladylike'. This acts as a punishment, and the child learns not to behave in that particular way. Skinner, in direct contrast to Freud, challenged the idea of human 'agency', believing that human states of mind do not 'cause' behaviour. For Skinner inner processes such as thinking and feeling are only 'responses' to the external world.

Behaviour modification based on the theory of operant condition-ing is a method of helping someone change undesirable and antisocial behaviour by offering rewards or punishments. For instance children with learning disabilities often respond favourably to being cuddled or given sweets, and if they wash themselves or go to the toilet at the right time, they can be rewarded in that way. They learn to modify and adapt their behaviour as a means of obtaining the reward. CBT represents a more sophisticated approach to behavioural and cognitive change and works through enabling the individual to unlearn patterns of depressive or negative thoughts. This is particularly useful for changing the way depressed people see their observation of other people's behaviour. By watching other people individuals witness the consequences of their actions and the behaviour that they assess to be appropriate under certain conditions. It is worth noting that although the results of these and similar experiments remain valid, the methodologies, using trickery and deception, are no longer permissible for ethical reasons.

Cognitive-developmental psychology

Cognitive-developmental psychology, an offshoot of cognitive psychology, developed as a reaction to behaviourism which, its advocates believed, ignored 'what goes on inside the heads' of human beings. Cognitive-developmental psychology therefore attempts to explore the maturational changes in mental structures as well as the changes in capacities which occur as the infant becomes the child and then the adult. This is a particularly relevant approach when considering aspects of socialisation (the way culture is transmitted from one generation to the next) as well as psychological development. Cognitive-developmental psychology is concerned with the way people process information derived from both their internal world and the external world, and the way in which changes in the processing mechanisms occur.

The most influential psychologist in the area of cognitive development was Jean Piaget, the Swiss research biologist, who, because he was writing in French from the 1930s, was not taken seriously until his work was translated to English in the 1950s. Piaget demonstrated that a child's behaviour alone did not present a complete picture and that the quality of the thought processes behind that behaviour needed equal consideration. Also he found that children of different ages had different ways of thinking and solving problems. Piaget's approach challenged thinking which at the time had been geared to intelligence-testing and quantifying changes in development.

The central idea of Piaget's work, and that of subsequent cognitive-developmental psychologists, is that every child is born with certain strategies for interacting with the environment. These strategies, which enable babies to make sense of their world in a particular way, are the starting points for the development of thinking. As children develop, so do their strategies – partly as a result of maturation, and partly as a result of the child's encounters with the external world. The discoveries the child makes about the world come about during the processes of development and exploration and occur in particular sequences. Thus there are certain things children are unable to do until they have grasped concepts which precede them (e.g. a child cannot grasp the idea of adding and subtracting until she has realised that objects are constant).

Piaget considered that the environment in which the child lives may affect the rate at which she goes through this developmental sequence, because the quality of experience is an important source of stimulation and mental exercise. However, as far as he was able to demonstrate, the environment does not enable children to miss out or skip stages in cognitive development. An understanding of the concept of children's cognitive structure is especially important for residential workers faced with the task of ensuring that the children in their care make sense of their worlds, and the reasons why they are in care. It also provides a means of assessing children's responses to particular situations, as in the case of 'good' and 'bad' behaviour and moral reasoning.

Piaget's interest in moral rules has a resonance with contemporary concerns about respect for others and unruly or disruptive behaviour of children and adolescents in schools and in public places. Typical assumptions are that young people who are disruptive will change their behaviour if they are threatened with punishments such as community service orders, where they might have to clean streets and public toilets under the supervision of probation workers or work on older people's gardens. This may not necessarily be the most helpful means of changing 'antisocial' behaviours. Piaget (1932) and Lawrence Kohlberg (1969) worked on this aspect of moral develop-ment. Piaget had based his research on younger children's thinking about intent in moral issues. He worked with children aged between 6 and 12 and told them pairs of stories about childish transgressions, asking them which action was the naughtier and why. The pairs of stories might be as follows:

(1) There was a little boy called John, who thought he would help his mummy by cleaning the kitchen. While he was doing this he knocked a pile of plates over, and they all broke.
(2) William's mummy told him never to play in the kitchen when she was not there, but one day he did, and knocked over a cup and cracked it.

Piaget asked, 'Who was the naughtier and why?' Younger children usually insisted that John was the naughtier because the consequences of his action were more severe. Piaget found that they did understand that he was trying to help, but were still more concerned about the amount of damage. He calls this type of reasoning 'objective responsibility', meaning that actions are judged on the basis of their material outcome rather than their intent. He also demonstrated that children's first views grow out of their relationship to adults as authority figures. They are subordinate to adults, and believe that rules emanate from sources *outside* themselves, which adults recognise and thus forbid and punish. He refers to this stage as 'heteronomous morality'. When children grow older, free themselves from adult authority and mix more with their peer group, they begin to understand that rules are social agreements, accepted by all members of a group as a basis for cooperative action. He refers to this stage as one of 'autonomous morality'. This suggests therefore that simply punishing young people for antisocial transgressions will not change their behaviours because they still think about rules in the same way.

In the late 1960s Kohlberg built upon Piaget's work on moral development. He aimed to show that, if cognitive development in human beings had a natural and normal development course, then moral reasoning may also demonstrate a normal pattern of development. This was based on the premise that if the development of moral reasoning demonstrates a standard or universal form of development with increasing maturity, then the mature form of moral thinking can be considered to be better or more desirable than earlier forms of moral thought. Kohlberg attempted to describe the changes in children's moral thinking systematically as they occur with development. He made a series of comparison studies of children of different ages, and a longitudinal study of a group of children as they grew up. The consistencies between these two studies gave him a firm basis for claiming that age-group differences do reflect individual development in moral reasoning.

Kohlberg presented his participants with a moral dilemma which contained a conflict between competing claims for justice. Their task was to choose a solution and explain their choice. After analysing the statements of children at various stages of development, he constructed a model of growth in moral reasoning. This consisted of three levels of morality, each of which could be divided into two stages, as in Table 1.1.

Table 1.1 Kohlberg's stages of moral reasoning

Level 1 Preconventional morality

The level of most children under the age of nine, many adolescents, and some adult criminal offenders.

Stage 1 The individual at this stage conforms to avoid punishment from authority, whose power she/he accepts.

Stage 2 Self-interested exchanges. Individual conforms to get the most possible advantage for himself/herself.

Level 2 Conventional morality

Most adolescents and adults are at this level. The individual now understands, accepts, and upholds social rules and expectations, especially those that emanate from authorities.

Stage 3 Maintaining good interpersonal relationships. The individual wants to be seen as good, and to live up to others' expectations. She/he will experience shame if seen in an unflattering light by important people.

Stage 4 Maintaining the social system. The individual agrees to a set of rules and obligations which are seen as justified in order for the system to operate.

Level 3 Postconventional morality

Only a minority of adults reach this level, and then rarely until they are 20 or above. Individuals at this level internalise their own formulation of society's rules according to their own moral principles. When a person's principles are at odds with social rules, the person will be guided by their own.

Stage 5 Social contract and individual right. Social rules are seen as capable of being changed by those affected. A revolutionary leader might operate at this stage.

Stage 6 Universal ethical principles. Individuals recognise the universal ethical principles to which they have a sense of personal commitment. Compliance is based upon personal conscience, not external pressure or even social contract. A martyr, or a terrorist, willing to sacrifice their own life for their cause might be seen to operate at this stage.

Kohlberg suggested that these levels of morality reflect three different social orientations. Preconventional people have a concrete individual perspective on society; conventional people have a member-of-society's view; and postconventional people take a prior-to-society perspective. Only postconventional people ask themselves what kind of social regulations a society would have to develop if it were to start from scratch. It is likely that the majority of social workers see themselves as operating at a postconventional level of moral reasoning which is necessary to work with people with very different moral rules, behaviours and experiences from their own. Social workers need to be more than tolerant 'liberals'. If they are going to work successfully with service users of all ages and backgrounds to help them change their behaviours then they need to be confident in their own, independent judgements of morality beyond those of popular rhetoric, policy and law enforcement. This does not mean that psychologists are advocating challenges to the current policy, law and social structures. It simply means that social workers, to do their work with service users effectively, need to be able to think beyond the popular imagination.

Kohlberg predicted that moral reasoning was related to behaviour. He did a series of experiments to show that people at a high level of moral reasoning are less likely to administer shocks in experiments like Milgram's (Chapter 6). Another piece of work which used Kohlberg's stages showed that children at stage 3 are more likely to give way to group pressure than those at a higher stage. Also, that people at stages 5 and 6 were seen to be more likely to cheat than those at 3 and 4. Another study showed that university teachers of science and university administrators tended to employ law-and-order reasoning more than social science and humanities teachers.

Carol Gilligan (1982/1993) provided a challenge to this view on moral reasoning, arguing that Kohlberg's model was 'gendered'. Through her own examination of moral stories which focused on matters like abortion – clearly of more immediate concern to girls and women – she found clear gender differences in the processes of reasoning with decisions made along lines reflecting the interests of each gender group. That is not to say that women and men came down on separate sides, or even the same sides as each other, when addressing issues around 'a woman's right to choose' an abortion. Gilligan found that they based their judgements on different premises.

Social psychology

Social psychology has origins in sociology as well as psychology, with Auguste Comte in France and Charles Cooley in America (at the turn of the 20th century) both making reference to 'social psychology'. The 1930s and 1940s were another period of growth with studies of industrial management and army leadership inspiring researchers. Social psychology is different from the approaches described so far, partly because it incorporates a variety of psychological theories, but especially because it focuses upon the study of more than one person, and of individuals within the context of wider social groupings. Most recently it has identified itself overtly with critical approaches to the discipline (Gough and McFadden, 2001).

Social psychology is important for social workers most obviously because of mutual concern for social networks. In Chapter 6, aspects of group behaviour relevant to understanding family patterns and institutional life are examined, while in Chapter 7 there is a discussion of the social psychology of social work organisations.

Social psychology is both responsive to, and initiates change in, conceptual and methodological issues. In the 1970s there was a direct challenge to the positivist model of research (Harré and Secord, 1972) arguing that an understanding of the deeper levels of human encounter could only be assessed through analysis of subjective accounts of actions rather than objective measurement of inter-personal behaviour. This line of attack upon mainstream psychology has been maintained and indeed strengthened through the work of social constructionists who argue for the understanding of human behaviour through the way individuals position themselves within existing discourses. This approach attempts to explain human experience (subjectivity) as an ideological venture rather than an essentially biological one, and so human social and individual actions might be understood as deriving from dominant social values rather than individual desires (see Gough and McFadden, 2001). This perspective is particularly important for social work practitioners grappling with the reasons why particular people appear to persist in what seem to be inappropriate behaviours.

The phenomenological or humanistic approach

Humanistic psychology was initially rooted in the optimism of the 1960s and the work of Abraham Maslow, George Kelly and

Carl Rogers. Rogers' work in particular was derived from his therapeutic/counselling work and, like Freud, he developed a theory of personality and human development based on his clinical experience (see Chapter 3). Unlike psychoanalysis however, humanistic psychology emphasises the positive nature of human beings and their efforts towards growth and self-actualisation or self-fulfilment.

Humanistic psychology stresses the importance of freeing individuals from any barriers within themselves and between the self and the external reality. It also differs from other approaches in psychology, because of the value it attaches to subjective experience – that the individual's own view of the world is reality. The main concern therefore is how people perceive themselves and their surroundings, rather than their behaviour.

The central component of Rogers' theory is the self-concept. Someone with a positive self-concept views the world quite differently from someone whose self-concept is weak. The self-concept does not necessarily reflect reality – someone may be successful in the eyes of others, but see him/herself as a failure. Rogers suggests that individuals have an 'ideal self', the person they would like to be, and that self-concepts of 'fully functioning' people are consistent or congruent with their thoughts, experience and behaviour (Rogers, 2002).

Evolutionary psychology

Evolutionary psychology has gained an enthusiastic response from the popular press over recent years because it appears to provide a watertight and scientifically-based rationale for gender–power differences and differences in gender-typed behaviours. It is based on the premise that human behaviour originates from natural selection, that is, the desire and behaviour by both males and females to maximise their reproductive potential. By definition, the strategies that men and women apply are distinct from each other because women have greater investment in an individual offspring (since each infant has a nine-month gestation period). By contrast, men can produce children each time they have sexual intercourse with a different woman. Thus it is argued that women have evolved to become sexually/socially shy and 'choosy', while men have to compete with each other through aggression in order to impregnate the 'best' female they are able. Hence the evolution of sex-typed personality traits. This work, usually developed through experimental means with humans (mainly students), is controversial within psychology and among feminist scholars, with the emphasis on sex differences in 'mating behaviour'. It owes its significance at the moment, at least in part, to developments in understanding the structure and influences of genetics on behaviour but the ethos of evolutionary psychology, which is essentially conservative, contrasts sharply with the values underlying social work practice. For social workers, though, there are important questions to be considered which evolutionary psychology has raised. For example, what would make an individual care for members of the family who no longer have reproductive potential such as parents or grandparents? Is altruism in general an evolved behaviour? Why do so many men appear to physically and sexually abuse their female partners and/or their children? These questions are beyond the scope of this book but are socially and politically important and need consideration. There is an ongoing debate (Rose and Rose, 2000; Campbell, 2002; Baron-Cohen, 2004) about the relevance and validity of evolutionary psychology.

Social work and psychology

A knowledge of psychology and the ways it can be applied are integral to effective social work practice. What therefore do social workers need to know?

1. Social workers need to know how to develop, reflect on and improve the psychological skills most useful in interviewing, providing therapeutically-based support and in assessing service users' needs. We shall be covering these issues in depth in Chapters 3 to 6.
2. Social workers need a thorough knowledge of human behaviour, including its relationship to motivation, personality and development in order to understand service users, colleagues and themselves. Personality and motivation are discussed in Chapter 5, psychological development through the life course in Chapter 2.
3. Similarly social workers need to be able to make sense of social care and allied organisations in order to cope with their own career or professional development and training requirements. This will be discussed in Chapter 7.
4. Social workers need information about applied research evidence on relevant topics, to be able to select what is relevant and apply it to the needs of service users and the organisations in which they work.

5. Social workers need to have enough knowledge of professional psychology to provide an effective and complementary service alongside clinical, educational and counselling psychologists and particularly to understand brief psychological therapies that have become widely used over recent times such as CBT (cognitive behavioural therapy) and CAT (cognitive analytic therapy).

Conclusions

It is because social work practitioners acknowledge the need to have access to scientific information about human performance, human development, pathology and so on, that psychologists have been asked to conduct research into these areas. The fact that social workers are being asked to place people with learning disabilities and long-term mental health service users in the community means that research into normalisation and stress in the family is funded. Finally, as social workers are having to account for themselves and re-evaluate how they spend their time, psychologists are being commissioned to evaluate a number of programmes run by local authorities and other social work agencies.

The relationship between psychology and social work then is highly productive but demands mutual respect and awareness. For social workers to ignore psychology or to take it for granted will lead to inadequate knowledge and practice. Similarly psychologists involved in teaching social workers or doing research into areas of social work need a detailed and sympathetic knowledge of the social work role.

---

putting it into practice

1 List the costs and benefits of using video links to interview children about abuse.

2 Make a checklist of psychological considerations that need to be taken into account before meeting the only survivor injured in a serious traffic accident.

3 Write a brief account of how you would write up a report of a meeting with the survivor of the road accident who is suffering from PTSD from (a) a psychoanalytic perspective and (b) a social learning perspective.

Further reading

Baron-Cohen, S. (2004) *The Essential Difference*. Harmondsworth: Penguin.

Orbach, S. (1999) *The Impossibility of Sex*. Harmondsworth: Penguin.

These two books are easy to read but each demonstrates a very different perspective on the psychology of human behaviour. Orbach concentrates of the application of intuition, feelings and emotion to understand interaction. Baron-Cohen looks at the day-to-day relevance of experimental psychology from an evolutionary perspective to look at gender relations, particularly the differences in behaviours and attitudes of women and men.

2 | Psychological development through the life course

Introduction

Here we explore the contributions of psychology to understanding the human life course. We do this selectively to demonstrate key illustrations for social work intervention. We begin by looking at attachment behaviours and how these represent the need we have for emotional relationships all through our lives and how the quality of early relationships impacts upon us. We then examine crises in development and finally integrate theories of attachment, loss and life crises to a model of psychological development that integrates multiple perspectives on psychology (see Chapter 1) and is of value to social work theory and practice.

Influences on development

Human development comes about through a mixture of biological, psychological, emotional, cognitive, social and cultural influences. Until relatively recently psychologists concerned themselves more with the developmental stages from infancy to adolescence, than on phases of adulthood. Research studies of adulthood tended to be studies of 'ageing', exploring the loss of memory and intellectual functioning conceptualised as deterioration rather than development. However, as evidence increasingly failed to demonstrate significant decline of intellect and memory in older people for reasons of age alone, there has been a shift towards seeing adulthood and ageing as part of a life course trajectory through which development and change occur (Holland, 1995; Holland et al., 1996). Other psychologists similarly have written about the female menopause and women's ageing as a phase of life rather than a clinical condition and the 'end' of fertility (see Gannon, 1992, 1999; Ussher, 2006). Men's experiences and perceptions of mid-life have also been explored as developmental phases rather than examples of decline (Boul, 2003) and sexual health and sexuality have been discussed as normal characteristics of growing older (Gott, 2005).

Contemporary developmental psychologists considering the experience of getting older have taken up debates about more general aspects of adulthood and ageing such as personality and maturity and their impact on the thinking and behaviour of older people (e.g. Sheldon and Kasser, 2001). Whether people continue to develop in positive ways throughout their lives is now the focus of attention with some researchers still arguing that older people's perspectives on life shrink with age (Herzog et al., 1982) although this may be more to do with the losses and limitations that older life presents than growing older per se (Pfeiffer, 1977). This indicates policy and practice implications challenging social isolation and limitations in day care and health facilities (Chapter 8). Overall contemporary psychologists consider adulthood through the lens of individual differences now rather than highlighting correlations of age and function as they did twenty years ago (e.g. Belsky, 1999).

A helpful way to understand and explore human development, changes and crises through the life course is that of 'identity'. Identity is the means through which we understand our past life and integrate experiences into our sense of who we are, or 'self', and through this integration we can also have expectations of our futures. Identity also enables us to bring together our gender, ethnicity, socio-economic status, relationships and unconscious elements of experience into the strengths individuals can build upon to survive. Symptoms of PTSD described in Chapter 1 are exacerbated because the trauma has in some way disrupted our sense of who we are. People who have become traumatised have less personal resources to survive emotionally if they have no memories of the events. The controversial debate about recovered memories has hindered mental health practitioners working to enable victims of abuse or accident to recover memories of their experiences. (There is evidence that some service users might have 'recovered' false memories of abuse. This has cast doubts on cases where trauma was so intense that individuals defended themselves against remembering the event and therapy enabled them to recover their memories and move beyond their PTSD.) It is important for people to be able to draw on their sense of identity particularly in times of crisis as integration of experience provides the chance for healing (Chapter 1).

The life course approach: integrating perspectives

Psychologists and other social scientists increasingly refer to theories of the life cycle, life span and life course. The term 'life cycle' is less frequently used in contemporary scholarship because of the implication that nothing changes – that one generation replicates the patterns of previous ones, although evidence suggests that to deny this may be wishful thinking (see Chapter 8). However these terms are used interchangeably in many texts, and models that show change through life and indicate the relationship of particular biological ages or stages of life to psychological and social changes and development are perennially useful for practitioners.

Erik Erikson's (1968) model of the life cycle (frequently referred to as the Eight Ages of Man) explores change through a series of crises which move people from one stage of psychosocial development to the next. Successfully overcoming these crises equips an individual with the skills and knowledge to cope with the subsequent demands of the next stage of life. Central to his theory is the negotiation of a viable identity that enables the individual to progress towards forming mature intimate relationships. Erikson believed that, provided a person is aware and reconciled to the strengths they have gained through the challenges throughout their life, they will be able to face old age and death without fear.

Psychologists now consider the whole of life as a platform for development although they still concentrate research and theory on specific processes (e.g. cognitive development, sociability) and from different perspectives (e.g. evolutionary psychology, psychobiology).

Reflexivity and the 'self'

Social developmental psychologists suggest a wider view that embraces theories from sociology, including socialisation and the transmission of culture across generations, symbolic interactionism and the more recent emphasis on (auto)biography as both an approach to understanding ideas like identity and as a research method (Roberts, 2000). Symbolic interactionism, initially based on the work of G.H. Mead in the 1930s, regards the role of 'others', including both those with whom we have close contact and our sense of 'society' (other people, social norms and so on) as crucial to our development. They are symbolised and given a meaning.

How do we come to understand our 'self' at any moment in time? How do we (as social workers or service users) account to our self for who we are and what we do and thus to other people? In order to address this we move away from psychology itself to explore the recently developed links between sociology and psychology to investigate the ways that individuals make sense of themselves in a social and biographical context. We all conceive of our (developing) self through the process of 'reflexivity' which Mead explains as the ability to think about ourselves in an objective way – as if we were making sense of who we are from the perspective of others – or at least from the perspective of how we understand and give meaning to those others, and envision how they make sense of the world. The reflexive process enables human beings to make sense of their actions and the context in which these actions occur – the immediate context and the context of the individual's life history. According to Mead (1934/1967) reflexivity is 'the turning back of the experience of the individual upon himself [sic]' and thus the individual is able 'to take the attitude of the other toward himself ... consciously to adjust himself to that process, and to modify the resultant of that process in any given social act in terms of his adjustment to it'. This is akin to 'having a conversation' with your self. So for example, the unnamed feeling someone might have of lacking energy, seeing life and the world pessimistically is also experienced by that individual, in the attempt to make sense of the experience, as if through the eyes of another. This means the individual can in some way 'witness' his/her own actions/feelings and identify them (perhaps) as 'depression'. A young person who wants to come out to his parents as gay will have a conversation with himself based on his experience of presenting himself in the world and presenting himself to his parents and how he thinks his parents see him and will then see him in this potentially different way. He will be coming out in the context of who he is and who he has related to – it will be part of his life, albeit a 'crisis' point in his developing identity and in his biographical context.

This series of conscious actions relies upon (auto)biography and past experience and also upon an understanding of social institutions and the cultural context in which a person lives and has lived. It is through reflexivity in this way that biography and self are created and recreated. Peter Ashworth (1979) suggested that there were two fundamental elements to the self in Mead's work: the knower and the known. This distinction recognises the structure of the conscious self. Mead equates these terms to the 'I' and the 'Me'.

Mead (1934) drew a distinction between consciousness and self-consciousness in human experience which is useful for understanding internal 'conversation' and reflexivity. He was particularly interested in the way social interaction and the internalisation of how we see significant others evaluating our behaviour and beliefs, influenced our self-conscious thoughts, and how those in turn were produced as a result of reflecting upon our consciousness. Thus:

> I talk to myself, and I remember what I said and perhaps the emotional content that went with it. The 'I' of this moment is present in the 'me' of the next moment. There again I cannot turn around quick enough to catch myself. I becomes a 'me' in so far as I remember what I said. The 'I' can be given, however, this functional relationship. It is because of the 'I' that we say that we are never fully aware of what we are, that we surprise ourselves by our own action.
> Mead, 1934/1967: 174

In other words, in order to be reflexive we need to see our self as the 'object' of thought (i.e. 'me') but the seeing is done by 'I', the subject. The 'I' is impulsive and unorganised and equates to Freud's id, while the 'me', having come under social constraints, enables us to experience ourselves 'objectively' and account for our feelings and behaviour in a socially recognised way. Thus we can experience ourselves 'objectively' (the me/known) by the part of ourselves that is doing the experiencing 'subjectively' (the I/knower).

Pure experience is impulsive, but, via a process of reflexivity, the self as object becomes socialised. This cursory consideration of the composition of the self does not explain continuity of experience which is important for understanding how the self/identity develops and how actions and events (such as divorce, having a baby, experiencing a bereavement or personal trauma) take on a meaning within the context of self.

Symbolic interactionists, following Mead, saw self and society as interrelated in that 'society' predated 'mind', and 'mind' was the result of interaction between the individual and the social world. It is not relevant here to develop a critique of that view. Here we draw attention to the indivisibility of the social and the self to develop an explanation for why a crisis in a person's life cannot be separated from either the individual experience or the cultural experience.

Biography and the life course

The phenomenological sociologists and psychologists of the 1960s were concerned to explain human experience in terms of individuals making their own sense of the world through the experience of constant interaction.

Experiences at each stage of our lives are given subjective meaning, and the meaning itself will have been interpreted and incorporated into our accumulated biography; that is, '[t]he common sense view ... that we live through a certain sequence of events, some more and some less important, the sum of which is our biography' (Berger, 1966: 68). Thus the biography is experienced and understood within a prescribed social context:

The socially constructed world must be continually mediated to and actualised by the individual, so that it can become and remain indeed his world as well. The individual is given by his society certain decisive cornerstones for his everyday experience and conduct. Most importantly, the individual is supplied with specific sets of typifications and criteria for relevance, pre-defined for him by the society and made available to him for the ordering of his everyday life. This ordering ... is biographically cumulative. It begins to be formed in the individual from the earliest stages of socialisation on, and then keeps on being enlarged and modified by himself throughout his biography.
Berger and Kellner, 1964, quoted in Anderson, 1982: 303

The notion of biography therefore enables researchers and practitioners drawing upon theory and research to take account of present and past considerations of how people account for their lives, while individuals give meaning to their lives within a socially prescribed framework, which includes a sense of social organisation and structure including gender.

As illustration we draw on a case study of Sally, a 27-year-old mother who was the victim/survivor of physical abuse from her partner and father of her baby. She had left him after following up on a prosecution (resulting in a fine) and was now receiving threats from him via his friends in the neighbourhood. During her initial interview it was clear that Sally had had two previous abusive partners, and although this did not prevent her being fearful it did make her feel more confident that she knew what to do by way of seeking assistance and what her rights were in a criminal justice and legal framework. There was some sense in which Sally knew she had a place in the world as a survivor in the context of domestic abuse. It also emerged that her father had regularly attacked her mother when she and her siblings were children resulting in them being taken into care and her mother admitted for psychiatric care. She went to live with her maternal grandparents when she was eleven and during the five years she was there she was sexually abused by her grandfather who beat up her grandmother relatively regularly – something that had apparently taken place throughout their lives together. At 16 she went to live with her first violent boyfriend. Sally recognised that she was attractive to men, and often men who were 'alpha' males which made her feel very powerful. However they also made her feel trapped, vulnerable and depressed in the longer term because of the violence, although she managed to muster enough self-esteem to leave each one eventually. Sally believed that men were violent, women had to put up with it or leave the man but that the next man would be similar. To hold on to a man you had to be attractive but you also had to expect violence, abuse and jealousy. That was women's experience – at least it was Sally's and she could see no other way than that.

How could Sally make sense of her life enough to make changes and move forward? This complex biography is not so unusual. Sally was experiencing herself as an attractive sexual being but also as a vulnerable victim as she was separating from the adults who had brought her up at around the age of sixteen. She was, though, living in a social/cultural context in which she was a victim of abuse and unable to break away because the abuse had been perpetrated by the very adult(s) in charge of her care. Her mother and grandmother had been abused also and Sally had witnessed this. Her vision of femininity and women's lives was one in which you could only survive through not putting up with this type of behaviour, although paradoxically it was men of violence who were potential protectors. For Sally, to be supported meant changing her sense of self and she had to move from beyond being sexually attractive and the object of a man's desire and attention (positive and negative). She needed to move beyond her sense of accumulated experience which provided the cues and symbols through which she assessed her identity and future life prospects. She also had to re-examine her biography through the 'eyes' of someone other than herself or those to whom she had related up until the time of her intial interview. In addition, she had to re-examine her early experiences of trust, shame, autonomy and sense of identity.

Here we draw attention to the value of integrating approaches which can be applied to understanding service users at various stages of the life cycle. The framework for this approach is Erikson's model of psychosocial development that brings in both the unconscious and the role of biology, biography and adaptation. Erikson took Freud's model of psychosexual development, described in Chapter 1, for granted and built his theoretical framework accordingly. This approach is set against the social context of the immediate family and socio-economic and cultural influences and well as the 'body'. Through the body as mediator we gain a sense of identity that embraces gender and ethnicity.

As individuals mature biologically and cognitively/intellectually they experience and make sense of the world around them at all of these levels. Developmental crises occur, as Erikson indicates, so for example a woman in her thirties will be looking for a 'generative' experience which might be to have a baby or it might be for a career development. A thirteen-year-old boy will be struggling to understand who he is as his body rapidly changes and his parents or carers no longer offer the stability or the hostility and source of anxiety that they had done before. While crises are age/stage related each one comes with a particular characteristic based on earlier biographical features. For the child who had had a disrupted early life and failed to gain any sense of trust in other people, each crisis might result in an increased sense of failure. This might lead them to become violent in later life, to an addiction to drugs or alcohol or psychiatric difficulties. For someone like Sally the crisis was more complex as it seemed unrelated to a particular age or stage but more to a recognition of accumulated failures to resolve developmental crises.

For some, despite a poor start in life, it is possible to regain a sense of security from subsequent relationships – either personal or professional with a therapist or social worker who enables the person to recognise and address the issues that remain in her/his life but originate from unresolved crises from an earlier time.

We now explore the detail of how relationships form and are given meaning and provide meaning to our lives at different times and stages.

Table 2.1	Erik Erikson's psychosocial stages	
Age	Stage description	Emotional tasks
0–1	Basic trust versus mistrust	Will the infant trust the care-taker?
2–3/4	Autonomy versus shame and doubt	Mastery of walking and other tasks – will they cope?
4–5	Initiative versus guilt	Will the child's new skills lead to too many mistakes?
6–12	Industry versus inferiority	Will the child be able to deal with intellectual tasks at school?
13–18	Identity versus role confusion	Adolescence – who am I?
19–25	Intimacy versus isolation	Can I be successful in relationships?
26–40	Generativity versus stagnation	Can I be creative?
41+	Ego integrity versus despair	Does my life make sense?

Attachment in infancy

The first means of gaining a sense of identity is through our relationships with others and early relationships between infants and their carers often set a pattern for the types of relationships people have through their lives. Moreover these early relationships equip individuals with their sense of self-worth, emotional stability and the ability to love and care for other people. The way we understand the social and emotional world around us therefore is part of a continual dyamic based upon the interaction between ourselves, others and the way we make sense of ourselves in relation to others. Early relationships in life are referred to as 'attachments'.

Attachment relationships occur when an infant learns, or experiences, love and trust with another human being (usually the mother, father or a main carer) who in turn attends to his/her needs with warmth and affection (Marris, 1996). Understanding attachment is central to understanding the powerful influences of love and loss throughout our lives. Human beings are capable of forming strong emotional bonds with each other and indeed throughout our lives we seek such attachments and work to maintain them.

There is evidence that when a baby is not able to form a relationship with a caring adult for some reason (perhaps because the adult is absent, is unable to express affection or the care is shared by a number of emotionally distant adults as with a children's home) then the child becomes emotionally withdrawn and depressed. There appears to be a consistent need to seek physical comfort among human infants and research with monkeys has demonstrated how the lack of physical contact leads to emotional deficit and/or disturbance in infancy and in later life (Harlow, 1961).

Humans, primates and many other species are social in nature and there is evidence of a drive to seek close and secure company. Attachments across the life cycle have been explored through empirical studies (e.g. Ainsworth, 1996) and through observational and clinical studies (e.g. Bowlby, 1969/1982; Marris, 1986, 1996). There is evidence that human infants thrive the best the more secure their intitial emotional attachments. There is also evidence that older children, adolescents and adults whose early experiences were characterised by failed attachments (of varying kinds) suffered psychological consequences (e.g. Harris and Bifulco, 1996; Parkes, 1996).

Bowlby's (1969/1982) work on attachment and loss has also contributed to knowledge of the psychological effects of insecurity derived from social impoverishment in infancy. Although there are real concerns about the validity and reliability of the empirical source of Bowlby's theory, concepts of 'attachment', 'loss' and 'change' are important for understanding life-long human development and a crucial component of psychology for social workers (see Chapter 8 for a discussion of the maternal deprivation thesis).

Since Bowlby's early work in the 1940s, there has been a growing interest in infant attachment behaviour. Schaffer and Emmerson's (1964) longitudinal study of 60 infants in Scotland showed that by the age of eighteen months they were each attached to about three people. In the very early days the infants demonstrate what they call 'indiscriminant attachment' although they become wary of strangers by around six months. Rutter (1972) produced similar evidence and stressed that infants can form attachments to men. Tizard's (1975) study of children in their adoptive families demonstrated that it is frequently possible to overcome early emotional disturbance and separation with a stable, loving environment.

Separation

In the 1960s and 1970s, Ainsworth used a series of observations of children of various ages to demonstrate the ways in which a mother's presence or absence can affect a child's behaviour and emotional security. She created a series of 'strange situations' where an infant and mother were in a room filled with toys. A stranger would enter, and the mother would leave shortly afterwards, having allowed time for the stranger to be introduced. Initially children stayed close to their mothers in the strange room, but soon moved to the toys, returning intermittently to establish contact. When the stranger entered, the child moved towards the mother, perhaps even hiding behind her, but most children warmed to the new person and responded to her efforts to play. When the mother left, however, most children showed distress and became less involved with play. Ainsworth (1964) suggested that once children have been exposed to separation, they become sensitised in such a way that similar experiences are likely to be especially traumatic for them. Douglas and Blomfield (1958), however, had found that long-term ill effects generally followed separation only when it was accompanied by a change of environment. Their study was related to hospitalisation of children, which indicates that the ill effects may be associated with the context of the environment rather than the change itself.

Loss

Marris (1986) developed Bowlby's ideas while also borrowing concepts from Piaget. He sees grief as a response to loss of meaning, suggesting that it is provoked by all situations of loss, including social changes and any conditions which disrupt an individual's ability to make sense of his/her life.

Loss is a core concept in the development of the human psyche and closely related to work on attachment, which is connected to human emotional strength. Freud's work on bereavement, at the end of the nineteenth century, led him to argue that the expression of grief following bereavement was not only natural and acceptable, but highly desirable. It was important to cry. It was important not to maintain the Victorian stiff upper lip. To bury such fundamental feelings of anguish would distort recovery and prevent emotional healing. The loss would be buried in the unconscious and never resolved. Some of the after effects would be similar to what we now think of as PTSD (see Chapter 1). There is a difference between looking back at a period of mourning with sadness and even shedding a tear for the lost person, and having intrusive thoughts and dreams which cause anxiety. The latter is symptomatic of unresolved grief.

It is not only bereavement that leads to grief. Peter Marris (1986) has shown that moving away from home and changes in the structure of a community can lead to a grief reaction. The experience of being burgled also can, in some cases, lead to a severe grief reaction particularly if someone has lost items of great sentimental value or feel their once-loved house has 'let them down' (Nicolson, 1994).

The healthy grief reaction involves the recognition of the losses. Some people deny their loss – even when it involves the break up of a marriage for instance, or children leaving home – because they feel it helps them 'deal' with the problem. Many people do not want to acknowledge their emotional responses even to themselves because they see them as signs of weakness. These people bury their feelings, but feelings as fundamental as the response to loss do not go away that easily.

In order to look at this more closely, we shall consider a traditional model of bereavement and the grief reaction.

Bereavement

Bereavement most frequently occurs from late middle age onwards. This kind of bereavement is usually concerned with the loss of a long-term partner, but clearly the distress and grief are also acute for a child who loses a parent or sibling, for parents who lose a child, or for anyone who loses a close friend. Although most social workers are involved with the elderly bereaved, and the major studies are concerned with this group, it is not a condition exclusive to the elderly. Similarly many of the reactions in bereavement are similar to those originally described by Bowlby in relation to loss and separation between parents and young children.

The grief reaction

Psychologists and psychiatrists have long been interested in bereavement and grief. As early as 1917 Freud stressed the psychological importance of mourning after bereavement. Grief and loss produce a mixture of physiological and psychological reactions which are closely bound up with the social pressures concerning a change in status. These are often accompanied by financial problems, particularly in the case of a widow whose husband was breadwinner and who may well not be adequately insured or able to earn a living.

Evolutionary psychologists have suggested that grief has adaptive origins and is a means of maximising reproductive fitness (Archer, 1999). Bowlby (1980) and Parkes (1972) also favoured this perspective pointing out that a successful and healthy grief reaction enables the bereaved individual to engage in another relationship which is not the case with the person who remains absorbed in and attached to the dead person.

Thus it is understandable that Colin Murray Parkes (1972), who made a famous study of 22 London widows and has taken a special interest in the concept of bereavement, suggests that grief is an illness. He justifies this by saying that the emotional and physiological symptoms cause people to go to their doctors for help because they experience physical discomfort and disturbance of function. Also, he says that newly bereaved people are often treated as sick by the rest of society. They are expected to miss work, to be visited by relatives, and have others take responsibility for major decisions. However, Parkes says that bereavement can also bring strength and maturity, and if people cope with the 'challenge' of bereavement they may well change their view of the world and themselves. He described the stages of grief reaction, but shows that at each stage people are subject to a series of emotional conflicts and a variety of psychological reactions which have also been replicated by other researchers and clinicians (Archer, 1999):

● *Searching*. People experience 'pangs' of grief rather than prolonged pain, and will often cry out for their loved one. This reaction can begin within a few hours or days of the bereavement, and usually reaches a peak of severity within 5 to 14 days. Bowlby has called this the phase of yearning and protest. The bereaved person shows a lack of interest in normal life, and experiences a persistent, obtrusive search for the person who has gone. Most normal adults are fully aware that there is no point in searching for the dead person, but this does not prevent a strong impulse to search. Many experience illusions in which they see the dead person, or they will look for him/her in a crowd of people. Some people frequently return to the locations that were the favourite places of the dead to check whether or not they have really gone from them.

● *Mitigation.* When people experience intense pining, something often happens to mitigate the grief and pain. Parkes says that this consists of a sight or sound to give the impression that the 'search' is at an end. The commonest experience is that the dead person is nearby, and this provides a very comforting sensation for the bereaved. This experience was reported by 15 of the 22 individuals in Parkes' study. Also, many people experience hallucinations and dreams which include the dead person. They are often happy, but include the feeling that something is 'not quite well'. Other forms of mitigation include the bereaved person not believing the loss has occurred: waiting for the dead person to come home, or disagreeing with doctors and other relatives that the death has actually occurred.

Several people report a 'numbness' on receiving the news of death, and feelings of unreality, but these reactions tend to be transient. Many will try and avoid thoughts of the lost person, and avoid meeting people who might discuss him/her, or getting into situations which might be connected with the dead person. Two-thirds of Parkes' sample found themselves putting away photographs, and trying to fill their lives with new experiences. However, bereaved people do tend to be occupied by the thoughts of their loss, and are unable to sustain this avoidance. With the passing of time it becomes less necessary to deliberately avoid memories of the lost person.

● *Anger and guilt.* Anger is a normal component of grief, but it changes its form and expression as time passes. During the first month after bereavement anger appears greatest, with the expression of a great deal of emotion concerning why the dead person actually died. The people who are most angry are often those who are the most socially isolated. The recognition of the irrationality of their anger leads bereaved people to feel guilty at the way they have behaved.

Freud suggested that individuals frequently experience feelings of ambivalence towards a partner, which gives rise to a wish for the other's death. This is tolerable provided it is only a fantasy, but an individual needs a defence against this emotion once the wish has been fulfilled. Thus the bereaved person turns the anger inwards. Naturally, very few relationships are without a certain ambivalence, and Parkes found a high proportion of guilt due to these feelings in the people he studied.

● *Gaining a new identity.* Part of the process of maturity through bereavement and coming to terms with grief, is the gaining of a new identity. Initially the bereaved person might adopt the values and attitudes of the dead person. This is particularly common if the bereaved person inherits certain of the dead person's roles – for instance, a man who has lost his wife might adopt her attitudes towards child rearing. This becomes less important as the bereaved person grows in confidence and gains a new identity in his/her new role.

Bereavement cannot be expressed as a simple stress reaction. It includes psychological and physiological reactions, such as insomnia, anxiety, nervousness, loss of weight and appetite, despair and depression, but it also includes the process by which a person regains a status and role in society. The death of a spouse causes a change in social circumstances due to 'stigmatising'. Western society is still not accustomed to dealing with the bereaved, particularly after the initial shock and the funeral arrangements, so people who continue to suffer are seen as not quite normal or acceptable – they do not fit in. Another source of stress for the recently bereaved is that most couples have pooled financial, emotional and social resources, and so the person who is left alone is without all the functions provided by the dead person. During the process of bereavement an individual has to counteract stigmatising and return to 'normality'.

Problems of bereavement

The side effects of grief and mourning are related to the social disapproval directed against people who cannot join in with everyday life. Although, as Parkes suggests, grief can be seen as an illness, and is indirectly recognised as such in terms of time taken off work and extra help being provided, the pain of loss for most people extends beyond the normal time allowed for mourning. Many bereaved people feel unable to talk about their memories for a few weeks after the death, by which time friends and relatives are trying to persuade them to take a fresh view of life and look to the future, but mourning will probably not cease until they have been able to express grief and talk about the dead person from the distance that time can provide.

Self-help groups have come into existence over the last few years which enable bereaved people to meet others, compare experiences, and support each other, but it is often necessary for the bereaved person to be able to talk to someone exclusively about their loss, and by doing so set a pattern for re-establishing a life for themselves without the pain or guilt of an unresolved loss. Carole Smith (1982) has reviewed the research studies which looked at the scope for identifying vulnerable individuals and groups, and outlined those responses which may or may not facilitate recovery from the impact of the loss. The issues raised from these studies have led to a consideration of whether professionals should intervene (Currer, 2001).

Conclusions

It is effective mourning for any loss leading to integration and change which leads to psychological well-being, which is where social work intervention can help. For people to move successfully through the conscious and unconscious crisis points in their lives they need to be reflexive and enabled to reflect on their self in the context of their biology, biography and experiences in an objective way.

putting it into practice

1 *Observation study of a young baby and her mother or father (or other main carer).* Noting the age of the baby, describe how the baby reacts, or doesn't react, when the parent or carer picks her up, talks to her, plays with her. Make a list of what you think is relevant evidence to assess the quality of the infant–adult relationship. For example does the adult make eye contact? How long for? Does the baby respond? What significance do you attribute to these actions and others you identified and observed?

2. *Reminiscence work.* Interview a person living in a care home or attending a day centre with a view to helping him/her recall his/her past. How important is reminiscence for the mental health of an individual coming to terms with their 'biography' and evaluating their life?

Further reading

Parkes, C.M., Stevenson-Hinde, J. and Marris, P. (eds) (1996) *Attachment Across the Life Cycle*. London: Routledge.

This book includes a series of related chapters by different authors about the way that our relationships at different stages of our lives are influenced by our early attachment experiences. It demonstrates the need we have for attachment and the problems we face when attachments are broken.

Archer, J. (1999) *The Nature of Grief: The Evolutional and Psychology of Reactions to Loss*. London: Routledge.

This book looks at bereavement and loss showing universal and biologically based responses to losses.

Both books are easy to read and informative.

part 2 | **Interpersonal and practice skills**

3 | Interviewing and counselling

Introduction

Social workers talk and listen to a wide variety of service users, colleagues and others. You may, for example, be gathering sensitive information from a service user with complicated needs one moment and liaising with a health or housing professional the next. One or more of the people involved may be anxious, upset or angry. Some of these conversations, meetings and interviews go well, but in others the participants thought that the outcome could have been better in some way and felt baffled or frustrated by the lack of communication. This chapter reviews some of the skills and personal qualities involved in interviewing and counselling more effectively. For an in-depth discussion of the use of counselling and counselling skills by social workers see Seddon (2005).

The chapter is in four main parts:

1. *Preparation and supporting skills*: preparation, negotiating a 'contract', attending, paraphrasing, reflecting, silence and summarising.
2. *Challenging skills*: asking questions, advanced empathy, giving information and immediacy.
3. *Counselling*: the effectiveness of counselling, and a three-stage model of counselling.
4. Some *suggestions for coping* with difficult aspects of interviewing and counselling.

Considerable improvements in interviewing skill can be achieved relatively easily (Maguire, 1981), while counsellor training is more complex, harder to evaluate and much less studied (McLeod, 2003). For example, Maguire and Rutter were concerned with improving communications between doctors and patients, and in particular with the initial history, i.e. doctors gathering accurate and relevant information from a patient new to them. They began by studying videotapes of such interviews between senior medical students and patients and found numerous deficiencies – including failure to pick up cues, repetition (which at best is a waste of time), asking leading questions and acceptance of jargon (e.g. taking at face value a statement like 'I feel depressed'). The results were very clear: 74 per cent of the students were rated as poor or very poor at picking up verbal leads, while 24 per cent failed to discover the patient's main problems – and this with patients who were chosen as cooperative and articulate.

Maguire and Rutter's next step was to devise a training programme, a 45- to 60-minute individual tutorial for each student in which one of her/his interviews was replayed and discussed, and compared with the information which should have been obtained. A handout on interview structure and technique was also discussed with reference to the replayed interview. The training was evaluated by comparing the amount of relevant and accurate information obtained by trained and untrained students respectively. Again the results were very clear: the trained students obtained nearly three times as many relevant items of information. On this evidence, interviewer training is necessary, desirable and highly effective.

A criticism of Maguire and Rutter's approach is that it focuses on skills, which are relatively easy to measure, and neglects qualities, which are more important but also more complex and elusive. For example *empathy* can be defined as 'showing that you understand the other person's feelings and see their point of view' – with the emphasis on 'showing', and in a specific way; *genuineness* as 'being yourself' – though 'appropriately' rather than bluntly or unflinchingly; and *respect* as 'warm acceptance of the other person' – though some people respond best to a matter-of-fact kind of warmth. The comments after each brief definition hint at some of the complexities (Bayne *et al.*, 1999; Merry, 2002).

In addition, some central theorists are dismissive about a skills approach. For example, Rogers (1987) commented on training people to 'reflect feelings' (p. 39):

It does not describe what I am trying to do when I work with a client. My responses are attempts to check my understanding of the client's internal world. I wish to keep an accurate up-to-the-minute sensitivity to his or her inner searchings, and the response is an endeavour to find out if I am on course with my client.

Skills training is sometimes superficial, and interviewing and counselling are in some respects mysterious and not captured at the level of skills. A sense of timing for example is part of this artistic side, but the term 'timing' is more a question than an explanation. However, skills training and personal development can also complement each other, with the skills giving a more systematic framework for analysis, and the skills discussed in this chapter can both communicate qualities like empathy and respect and help to develop them. Conversely, using the skills without sufficient development of the qualities is likely to seem mechanical and hollow.

Using this chapter

This chapter helps you analyse your own interviews and other conversations in a constructive way. In this section the approach to this self-training and the meaning of 'constructive' are elaborated with some general principles and some suggestions about 'feedback'. The principles are:

1. Good use of the skills (and the quality of genuineness) implies individual style.
2. Everyday conversations give lots of opportunities for practising the skills, and some opportunities for observing them. They 'belong to life', as Egan put it, and are not magical (though their effects can seem so). Moreover, you are probably good at some of the skills already. The assumption here though is that all helping professionals, whatever their training and experience, can usefully review their skills.
3. Improvement may not happen all at once, or in a smooth progression. It may well involve feeling self-conscious and awkward for a while but, as with developing other skills (e.g. driving, playing a sport or cooking), the skills feel 'right' and natural in time. For most skills, it takes many years of practice and appropriate feedback to achieve virtuoso standard (Anderson, 2000). Fortunately there is improvement meanwhile, and it is not necessary to be a virtuoso to be effective.

To give 'feedback' is to comment to someone on how well you think she/he has done something. Here it refers more specifically to commenting on how well or not the person has communicated core qualities and used supporting, challenging, assertive and stress management skills.

The following principles are general guidelines; as with counselling there are no absolute rules. Moreover, giving feedback is itself a skill, and therefore develops with appropriate practice.

● Comment on behaviour, and try to be fairly specific, e.g. 'I seemed very relaxed – I think it was the way I sat and my use of silence.' (The comment could be more specific still, but this is probably sufficient.)
● Include positive comments.
● Criticise behaviour that could be changed and try to say what you might do differently: one or two changes at a time only.
● Be brief.

Preparation and supporting skills

Supportive skills can be used with the emphasis on gathering information (interviewing) or on helping someone clarify and explore (counselling). The skill of asking questions is in the section on challenging skills but could arguably be included here. It is central to some approaches to counselling and obviously to interviewing. However, in terms of the model of counselling discussed later, although questions can be supportive (and occasionally empathic) they are usually challenging.

Preparation

Preparing for an interview can include thinking about the following factors: the time available, what you hope to achieve, whether your aims conflict with those of others, such as organisations, a broad structure for the interview, and what information might be useful. A straightforward structure would be 'Introduce myself. Find out about X. Find out about Y. Agree on action.' A structure is a checklist of aims and topics, and perhaps an opening question for each topic. The possible aims include gathering information (for one or more specific purposes), giving information, helping someone to make a decision or to behave differently. There is also a 'public relations' element. The term is perhaps unfortunate, but how social workers are seen by service users matters because it affects whether they see you in the first place, how much they trust you and whether they continue to see you.

Clearing your mind of distractions is another aspect of preparation, aiming for what Michael Argyle called an 'atmosphere of timeless calm'. Relaxation exercises are one possible way of approaching somewhat nearer to 'timeless calm' than normal, for example this breathing exercise:

1. First make yourself comfortable. Take two or three deep breaths through your nose. Then place one of your index fingers on the point between your eyebrows, with the thumb on one nostril, middle finger on the other.
2. Closing your left nostril, breathe in slowly and deeply through the right.
3. Closing your right nostril, breathe out slowly through the left.
4. Keeping right nostril closed, breathe in through the left.
5. Closing left nostril, breathe out through the right.

You can breathe in to (say) a count of three, hold for two, out to six – but ideally find your own rhythm. A further refinement of the instructions is that when you've breathed out, pause and wait until you want to breathe in, until it feels right.

This simple technique has not been tested experimentally yet. Benson (1977) described a similar procedure which has been tested and which, like many techniques, works well for some people. He sees it as meditation without the unnecessary trappings, and calls it the 'relaxation response'. The procedure is as follows:

1. Sit quietly in a comfortable position and close your eyes.
2. Deeply relax all your muscles, beginning at your feet and progressing up to your face, by tensing and relaxing each part of your body in turn or by 'playing dead'.
3. Breathe through your nose. As you breathe in say the word 'one' to yourself. Continue for 10 minutes. When you finish, sit quietly.
4. Do not worry about success in being relaxed: allow relaxation to occur at its own pace. Expect other thoughts. When they occur ignore them by thinking 'oh well' and continue repeating 'one'.
5. Practise this procedure once or twice daily, but not until two hours after a meal.

Physical relaxation is an obvious way of coping with stress, both immediately and preventively, and instructions/guidelines are widely available. Two ten-minute sessions of progressive relaxation a day seem to have a beneficial and cumulative effect (Seligman, 1995). However, sometimes, attempting to relax is itself stressful. Several factors can make a difference, e.g. some people prefer a well-lit room, others a dark one; some respond best to several two- or three-minute sessions, and so on (Lazarus and Mayne, 1990, cf. Rosenthal, 1993 on guided imagery, visualisation, pets etc.)

Further aspects of preparation are (again, ideally) having a quiet room with no interruptions, and knowing that the interviewee has waited, if at all, in pleasant surroundings. Such factors obviously do not guarantee a good interview, but they probably increase the chances of one. The interviewer might also consider what if anything she or he knows about the interviewee, and therefore what legislation, agencies and other resources are relevant.

Negotiating a 'contract'

Negotiating a contract is a useful early step in the interview itself. The contract is a concise statement about the purpose of the interview and a request for the other person's response or for what they see as the purpose. For example, 'I'd like to find out as much as possible about your experience with children. We have about 30 minutes. I'd like to take notes, which will, of course, be confidential. Is that OK?'. You might also say to the interviewee: 'Can you begin by saying why you've come to see me?', or 'What do you hope will happen as a result of this meeting?'. There may be a significant gap between what the interviewee expects and what the social worker can provide. Possible elements of the contract include: time available, place, number of meetings, resources, style/process, confidentiality, note-taking etc. It is vital to be clear about your own intentions, to listen very carefully, and for there to be genuine agreement before proceeding. Some elements may not be negotiable, so the skill is also concerned with setting boundaries.

The advantages of negotiating a contract are numerous. The interviewer is likely to become less mysterious and threatening. The ground is cleared and a purposeful tone is set. If agreement is genuine, both people are more likely to take part wholeheartedly. If you do not reach agreement, at least some time is saved.

In outline the basic skill is straightforward:

1. Say what you would like to do, etc. and/or ask the other person to say what he/she would like to do.
2. Listen.
3. Agree if possible. You or the interviewee may modify your perceptions or intentions in the light of the other person's intentions. The skill can be used for renegotiating or clarifying at any point in the interview.
4. Check the contract from time to time and be ready to renegotiate.

Attending

Attending is partly giving fairly straightforward non-verbal 'messages': looking at the other person, but not staring; being fairly relaxed; nodding slowly; smiling (if appropriate); not fidgeting. It is also partly internal: avoiding distractions and concentrating (hence the relaxation exercise). One problem with attention can be also a strength. The average rate of speech is about 125 to 75 words a minute, but we can think much faster. The difference can be used to daydream, to worry, to think about anything at all, or it can be used to attend to such questions as 'How is the relationship between you and your interviewee?', 'What is she/he not saying?', 'What about her/his non-verbal behaviour?', 'What about mine?', 'Where is the interview going at the moment?', 'Is this relevant to the aims?', 'Time to summarise?', 'Support or challenge?'.

Paraphrasing

All the skills outlined so far can have strong effects, out of all proportion to the way they appear. This is particularly true of paraphrasing (sometimes called 'basic empathy', restating, rephrasing or active listening). It is the single most powerful communication skill in most professional circumstances, because it is the main way in which empathy is communicated and because it clears up more miscommunications than any other skill. It is described here in detail. The idea is to *gradually* try out any aspects that are new and appealing.

A paraphrase is an attempt to restate, in a fresh way, the main part of what someone has said without adding any of your own ideas, feelings, interpretations, etc. The tone is slightly questioning without being a question, and your aim, in Rice's phrase, is 'to unfold rather than package experience' (Rice, 1974: 305). The most basic form of paraphrase is 'You feel ... [emotion] because...'. You therefore restate your understanding so far of your client's emotions and his or her view of the reasons or causes. It is far more than saying 'Yes, I see what you mean', or 'I understand how you feel' (which may mean 'I know how I feel in that situation').

A key element in good paraphrasing is being in close emotional contact with the other person and also clearly separate: neither overidentifying (sometimes called 'fusing') nor being coolly distant. Davenport and Pipes (1990) suggested the analogy of swimming close to a deep powerful whirlpool: 'the challenge is to be close enough to the emotional energy to understand what the client must be experiencing without getting swept down into the action oneself' (p. 139). Drowning with the other person is not helpful, nor is viewing from too far away.

A key practical question is 'How often should I paraphrase?'. The answer varies, but Rogers (1987) believed in frequent checks, and Gendlin (1981: 19) suggested an *average* of every five or ten sentences. Gendlin's suggestion can be treated too literally! It is a guideline, not a rule, and its merit lies in being concrete about the term 'frequent'. Gendlin made another specific suggestion about frequency: 'Don't let the person say more than you can take in and say back. Interrupt, say back, and let the person go on' (p. 20).

If you paraphrase well, the other person is more likely to either say more and go further 'inside' (may become more focused and intent), or sit silently, relieved that she/he has been understood and accepted. If you paraphrase less well, the other person is more likely to try to paraphrase what you've said, or become tense, confused or annoyed ('I've just said that'), or agree in a desultory way.

Three subtle aspects of paraphrasing well are that if you've understood (or think you've understood) only part of what the other person has said, paraphrase that part, and add that you don't understand the rest; to pause before you paraphrase or during a paraphrase, and trust yourself to find words which are good enough or better; and to try including a *little* of the other person's emotion or emotions in the way you say the paraphrase.

Perhaps the most difficult aspect to learn is accurately paraphrasing depth of emotion. Gendlin (1981) suggested successive approximations, gradually getting closer, as a realistic expectation.

'Accuracy' is defined at this stage by the other person: it is whether the paraphrase feels right to him or her that matters. This may well also be desirable: you gradually work together towards clarity rather than you being a therapeutic wizard.

A scale for giving feedback on paraphrasing of emotions is given below:

1. Communicated no awareness of even the most obvious emotions.
2. Slightly accurate about explicit emotions.
3. Often accurate about explicit emotions.
4. As level 3, plus slight accuracy about underlying, veiled emotions.
5. As 3, plus often accurate about underlying emotions.
(6. Flawless accuracy).

Paraphrasing at level 2 on this scale would probably be helpful to most interviewees, at least through the *attempt* to understand and listen without judging. Level 3 is reasonably empathic. Level 4 would be more helpful and level 5 a very high level of skill and an ideal to aim for. Level 6 is the aim of some interviewers, but is not realistic.

What other ways are there to help clients find the right words to describe an emotion? A technique that works well for some clients, but makes no sense to others, is to ask 'Can you say where in your body the feeling is?'. Locating it and then focusing on it can be clarifying. Another option is for the interviewee to repeat what they've said much more slowly, and perhaps more than once.

A further option is to use four broad categories as a first approximation and then refine them (Yalom, 1989; Bayne et al., 1999). The four categories are Sad, Mad, Bad and Glad. Although they are easy to remember, two of them are open to misinterpretation, so Sad, Angry, Afraid and Happy are alternative terms. Each of them can be refined, e.g. Angry could mean furious, fed-up, frustrated etc. In addition, emotions are quite often mixed, with, say, jealousy being both bitter (a variation of Angry) and upset (Sad) or affect-about-affect e.g. being afraid of anger.

A useful way of looking at paraphrasing is to contrast it with other kinds of response. For example, suppose someone says 'I feel so hopeless. My children don't listen. I've no money. My wife is hardly here and when she is she just sits or we argue. We don't go anywhere. I used to like going out with her.' (You may like to pause here and imagine a range of possible responses.)

The first eight responses listed below are *not* examples of paraphrasing:

1. To move on to another subject.
2. To say 'Nonsense', or 'You don't really mean that'.
3. To offer advice: 'If I were you ...' or 'What you could do is...'.
4. To sympathise: 'I know just how you feel ...', or 'I feel the same way sometimes ...', or 'Lots of people feel like that ...'.
5. To offer practical help: 'Why don't you come out with me?'.
6. To blame society etc.
7. To diagnose: 'When do you feel this way?' or 'How long have you been married?' or 'The main problem here is...'.
8. To attack: 'People like you ... You make me...'.
9. To paraphrase: 'You sound despairing, and sad about the way your life has changed so much'.
10. To reflect: 'Hopeless?' (gently).

What responses 1 to 8 have in common is that they do not encourage people to explore their thoughts and emotions further from *their* point of view. On some occasions these responses can be helpful but in a fundamentally different way from paraphrasing which says, in effect, 'I want to see your point of view, as a first step'. With enough practice, paraphrasing becomes at least as natural as offering opinions and advice, or asking questions, or other responses. It is natural in the sense that some people do it without formal training.

You may like to think of a similar range of responses to someone saying: 'The baby cried all night. I came close to hitting him. I want to have a life of my own. I'm so fed up', and: 'You're a lot of pompous do-gooders. I despise you. You're no use to anyone except your own kind. I don't know how you can live with yourselves, why don't you do a proper job?'.

Reflecting

The most useful meaning of reflecting is that it's to say back a word or phrase that your interviewee has used. The skill lies in timing, in using it only occasionally, and of course in choosing what to reflect. Used well, it is obviously economical and can be very effective.

A variation is the delayed reflection when you remember a phrase or word the person used earlier, and tie it in with something she/he has just said, but relatively gently and tentatively rather than as an interrogation. This can be a more challenging skill than paraphrasing.

Silence

Interviewers are sometimes afraid of silence and rush to fill the gap. Generally it is more skilful to wait, and try to assess why your interviewee has stopped talking. Reasons include:

● there is nothing more she/he wishes to say about a particular topic;
● to organise thoughts/look for the right word;
● to remember something;
● feeling angry, defensive, confused, etc.

The kind of silence (productive, peaceful, rejecting and so on) suggests which skill to employ: silence, a paraphrase, an open question, a summary or 'immediacy'.

Summarising

Summarising can help your interviewees (and you) clarify what they mean, feel and think. It may also increase their sense of control and hope. Summaries, like paraphrases, need to be tentative and, obviously, to outline what your interviewee has said so far. The implicit question at this point is: 'How accurate is it?'. If the relationship is good enough, your interviewee will probably tell you. When the summary is or becomes accurate, the question is: 'Where next?'. 'Where next' may be further general exploration, the end of your interview or a focus on one problem or aspect of a problem.

Three other skills for moving interviews forward can be very useful when your interviewee has several problems or a problem with several elements. More precisely, they each offer a way of moving forward.

The skills, adapted from Gilmore (1973), are called:

● Choice point
● Figure ground
● Contrast

Choice point is a summary plus an explicit question along the lines of: 'Is there one of these you'd like to talk about first?'.

Figure ground is when *you* suggest what to focus on first. 'Perhaps your main worry is ...?'. Sometimes it's best to focus on your interviewee's main worry, other times on something more straight-forward. Either way you still offer your interviewee the choice.

A *contrast* is a summary followed by a hypothetical question. It can work very well: your interviewee becomes clearer and more focused. On the other hand, it can be a premature and wrong solution and your interviewee can feel irritated by your superficial approach or feel demoralised. Much depends on the relationship between you and the interviewee, your timing and your manner.

The following example illustrates the three skills. Ola's partner has left him and their two children, aged 5 and 8. He is upset and frightened of the responsibility. His mother, who lives 100 miles away, has invited them all to stay with her, but Ola isn't sure. The children want to stay at home, near their school and friends. He hopes his partner will come back. He's also very worried about money.

Summary
Ola, you're very worried about what's best for your children and scared about what happens if your partner doesn't come back, but hoping she will. If she doesn't, money will be increasingly tight.

Choice point
Summary plus: Of all the things you've talked about – your relationship with your partner, maybe staying with your mother, looking after the children, money – which do you think we should look at first?

Figure ground
Summary plus: Perhaps the first thing for us to talk about is whether to stay with your mother or not?

Contrast
Summary plus: I wonder if it would be helpful for you to imagine what it would be like for your children at your mother's?

Challenging skills

Challenging skills introduce a new perspective on your interviewee's problems; they come from *your* frame of reference, from a way of looking at something or feeling about it which is different from the other person's. This is a fundamental contrast to supporting skills, which attempt to stay in the other person's frame of reference.

Asking questions

There are various categories of question but the most useful distinction is probably between open and closed questions. Open questions invite the interviewee to talk at greater length if she or he wants to, e.g. 'Tell me about X', 'What's happened?', 'Mmmm ...', and perhaps less obviously: 'In what way?' and 'Can you say how?'. They encourage the interviewee to give an overview, and thus the interviewer is likely to gather fuller information.

Closed questions on the other hand are easy to answer with one word. Moreover, a series of closed questions soon sounds like an interrogation, with the interviewee more likely to leave information out because 'I wasn't asked'. More subtly, in using a series of closed questions the interviewer is saying in effect, 'I know what is important and relevant. I will ask the questions. I will come up with a solution', when (especially in counselling) you are helping the other person to work on the problem. Open questions give space and involvement while closed questions help place the other person in a dependent, passive relationship, but both types of question generally come from the interviewer's viewpoint more than the interviewee's, thus hindering empathy.

Some examples of open questions are: 'What kinds of things have you tried?', 'When do you feel best about yourself?', 'What might happen if you did that?'. The most effective pattern, generally, is to ask one or more open questions on a particular topic, and then if necessary follow up with closed questions, e.g. to check a piece of information: 'Was that *two* or *three* months ago?'. 'Why' questions are open but may lead to the interviewee feeling attacked, or making up an answer to please you. (Like all 'rules' of interviewing this is only generally so.) Consider the difference between 'Why are you scared of going to the doctor?' and 'Can you say what scares you about ...?'.

Many other forms of question have been suggested, e.g. leading questions like 'I suppose you're sorry now?', which are both closed and suggest the 'right' answer. Simple and apparently trivial differences in wording can have dramatic effects. General principles for interviewers are to ask fewer questions, to prepare opening questions carefully, and to let what the interviewee says influence strongly any follow-up questions.

Advanced empathy

Advanced empathy is stating a hunch about how your interviewee is feeling or thinking when he/she seems to be unaware of it. This is risky. The risk is reduced by *earning the right* to challenge by empathising first, by challenging tentatively, and by returning to supporting skills immediately after challenging (i.e. you introduce a new perspective and then listen hard and actively to the other person's reaction).

Other challenging skills include *confronting* – suggesting themes or patterns, or someone else's point of view, or asking your interviewee how someone else sees it, or pointing to an apparent discrepancy; *self-disclosure* – revealing something personal with the intention of helping your interviewee or your relationship with them; and using a *technique* (Bayne et al., 1999).

Giving information

An important part of the skill of giving information is checking or putting aside your assumptions about people's knowledge, their ability to understand or remember the information, and their reaction to it. On the one hand, powerful emotions, selective memory, wishful thinking and information overload can make giving information futile. On the other hand, information can dramatically reduce distress and increase understanding. For example, I remember reading that my badly sprained ankle was equivalent to a broken one and at once feeling much more patient with how long it was taking to heal. My feelings of impatience and frustration were transformed by this new way of looking at my injury.

Ways of giving complicated information so that it is more likely to be remembered and acted on include: use simple words and short sentences, categorise explicitly, be specific (concrete), avoid jargon, repeat, check, and provide written back-up material (Ley, 1988; Nichols, 2003). Another strategy is to give your client a list of possible questions about the information to help her/him clarify what she/he would like to know (if anything).

Nichols (2003) reviews informational and emotional care. 'Emotional care' entails expecting people to feel anxious when threatened, angry when frustrated, sad about loss, and so on, and if they do, accepting it (mainly through the supporting skills reviewed earlier).

Immediacy

Immediacy is probably the most difficult challenging skill. One form of immediacy is talking about your experience of what is happening at that moment between you and your interviewee, and encouraging her/him to do the same. It is 'direct, mutual talk', and you are both involved; the focus is on you and the relationship rather than just on your interviewee. For example, 'I feel stuck, as if we're going round in circles. What do you think?', or 'I see us as playing something of a game. I think that I'm suggesting solutions, which may be much too soon, and each time I do, you point out why it won't work ...' (Bayne *et al.*, 1999; Egan, 2002).

Table 3.1 (overleaf) is a checklist for analysing your interviews. You may find it most helpful when used with the guidelines on developing skills and on feedback from the introduction to this chapter, and those on giving and receiving compliments and criticism from Chapter 4 on assertiveness.

Note that the checklist is a mixture of intentions and ways of trying to succeed in them. Your response to the checklist might combine evaluations – 'Yes, I did welcome my client well' – and comments on behaviour/skills – 'I used my client's name, I smiled (rather than beamed). I reflected the word "better" in her first sentence well, but forgot to agree to a time in the "contract" ...'

Then in your next interview, try to improve *one or two* aspects of your skills.

Counselling

Does counselling work?

It is very important, ethically and financially, to know how effective or ineffective counselling is. Do some approaches or methods actually do harm? Do some of the cheaper or quicker approaches work just as well as others? The answer to these questions appears to be 'yes' (Stiles *et al.*, 1986; Hubble *et al.*, 1999; DoH, 2001a) though there are still problems. For example, not much is known yet about *why* counselling works, or which elements and approaches are the most effective in which situations; there are more than 400 approaches to counselling, and only a few of them have been studied in any detail; and there have been thousands of studies of counselling, and several

Table 3.1   Checklist for analysing interviews

Preparation

Did I:

Plan the interview (e.g. decide about aim(s), structure, look up procedures, legislation)?
Prepare the seating etc.?
Clear my mind?

Did I:

Welcome my interviewee?
If a first meeting, introduce myself?
If necessary, attempt to put my interviewee at ease?
Negotiate a contract and set boundaries?

Did I:

Attend?
Help my interviewee talk both freely and to the point?
Follow up leads?
Check my understanding?
Help my interviewee to focus?

Did I communicate:

Respect?
Empathy?
Genuineness?

Did I end skilfully?

Overall

What state is my interviewee in now compared with at the beginning?
What about my style, e.g. warm, abrasive, obscure, formal?
Did I overuse any skills and neglect others?
What about pace?
Mannerisms?
Posture?
What state am I in?
Is there anything it would be helpful to do?
What of value did this interview achieve?
Are there any changes in my approach to try next time?

major reviews of the studies to try and make sense of the variety of counsellor, client, problem, method etc. involved.

There is also fairly general agreement that the main approaches work about equally well for most purposes. One reaction to this extraordinary position is that it is untrue, that some approaches have yet to be fairly tested or cannot be tested. A second reaction is to look for 'common ingredients'. If there are common ingredients, comparative outcome studies are 'costly experiments in futility' (Ahn and Wampold, 2001) and research on effectiveness should focus on clarifying the various possible common factors, especially the nature of the 'therapeutic relationship' and client readiness to change (Hubble *et al.*, 1999). Tallman and Bohart (1999) argue for two further implications: that the most important elements of counsellor training are intensive practice of listening and respect for clients' strengths.

A three-stage model of counselling

The rest of this section discusses a model of counselling or 'problem management'. Some problems cannot be solved in any complete sense, but all problems can be managed (Egan, 2002). As with the skills, the idea is for you to try out those parts of the model which make sense to you and 'fit' you, and to do this gradually and systematically, i.e. practice with analysis/feedback, as discussed early in the chapter. The model will either clarify part of what you do already, and perhaps crystallise it, or suggest new aspects of counselling to integrate into your own style.

The three-stage model of counselling outlined in Table 3.2 is broadly consistent with other widely used models, e.g. Dryden and Feltham (1992, in press), Egan (2002) and Hill (2004).

In Stage One, the counsellor uses supportive skills to help the client clarify, and to begin to form a trusting relationship. Stage One is sufficient for some clients: change of attitude, or a decision about what to do, emerges naturally, without further help.

Stage Two is, if necessary, offering new perspectives to the client, i.e. using challenging skills. The client may then see his or her problem differently, 'reframe' it, feel differently about it.

Stage Three is, if necessary, helping the client decide what to do, and to evaluate the results. Good goals are specific and realistic. Supporting and challenging skills are used throughout and taking small steps is a useful principle.

Table 3.2   A three-stage model of counselling

Stage One: Explore

The counsellor empathises with her or his client and is respectful and genuine. The client explores his or her emotions, thoughts and behaviour related to a problem.

Stage Two: Understand

If necessary, the counsellor suggests, or helps the client to suggest, themes, patterns, other ways of looking at the problem.

Stage Three: Action

If necessary, the counsellor helps the client to decide if any action is appropriate, and if so, exactly what, taking costs and benefits for self and others into account, and to evaluate the results.

The notion of small steps is related to another issue: how much change is possible? Smail (1987) argued that counselling is 'much less help than almost any of us can bear to think', but that this is *desirable:* we are not computers to be reprogrammed. Similarly, Zilbergeld (1983) suggested that we tend to hear only the dramatic success stories from counsellors and clients; that more often problems are reduced in intensity rather than 'cured'; that in any case many problems, e.g. depression, are best understood as normal human variation; and that recognising these limits to change can liberate a person to put energy into other things – 'I'm never going to be an X but what I can do well, and improve, is Y.'

The three-stage model is a guide, not a mechanical procedure. Thus, some clients present one problem clearly, others many confused problems at once. Some need only Stage One (or, more rarely, only a later stage), or Stage One for one problem, but all three stages for another, and so on. It is flexible for the style of counselling too. Each counsellor can give the model her/his own emphasis and flavour but, in general terms, the main value of the model remains: it *slows down* the way we normally respond to problems, with the aim of being more effective and saving time overall. It is thus impeccably logical –

indeed obvious – but not widely used. Instead, people tend for instance to think about actions before exploring their problem sufficiently or to be stuck and feel hopeless.

The model also provides a map and a framework. The map allows the counsellor to locate a particular point in the session or the purpose of a particular intervention, with implications for what to do next, and the framework can organise counselling techniques from other approaches, turning a haphazard eclecticism into a more systematic one.

Table 3.3 is a checklist for analysing a counselling session. The guidelines for using the checklist for analysing interviews (Table 3.1) also apply here.

Table 3.3   Checklist for analysing counselling sessions

Preparation

Did I:

Plan the interview? (But the client's aims are a strong priority)
Prepare the seating etc?
Clear my mind?
Negotiate or renegotiate a contract (if appropriate)?

Stage One

Did I:
Attend?
Paraphrase emotions?
Paraphrase content?
Summarise?
Use any of the other techniques for 'moving interviews forward' (if appropriate)?
Control the process (as opposed to the content)?

Stage Two (if appropriate)

Did I:
Earn the right (through being sufficiently empathic) to challenge?

continued overleaf

Table 3.3 continued

Stage Three (if appropriate)

Did I help my client:

Set workable goals?
Examine the consequences of achieving the goals?
Choose which goals to pursue?
Generate a variety of strategies?
Evaluate the strategies?
Decide on action(s)?

Overall:

How is my client?
Was I empathic?
Was I respectful (accepting)?
Was I genuine?
How was the balance between support and challenge?
Did I overuse any skills or neglect others?
What about pace?
What about mannerisms?
What about posture?
Which stage is each problem in?
What of value did this interview achieve?
Are there any changes to my approach to try next time?
What state am I in?
Is there anything it would be helpful to do?

Some difficulties and strategies

Some of the difficulties facing social workers when interviewing and counselling, and possible strategies for dealing with them, are briefly reviewed next. Much depends on personality and circumstances and there are different ways of responding well to someone who is angry, for example. Moreover, most of the suggestions have not been rigorously tested by research.

Many of the strategies are derived from skills discussed in the rest of the chapter. 'General purpose' strategies are to paraphrase, to use immediacy and to renegotiate the contract. Some general sources of advice and suggestions on interviewing and counselling are Yalom

(1989, 2001), Dryden and Feltham (1992, in press), Bayne *et al.* (1999) and Feltham and Horton (2006).

Referral. Referral is often ethically responsible. However, while it can be a relief, it can also be disruptive and disappointing, especially for people who have been passed from one agency to another. Referral should be seriously considered in circumstances when you don't have the relevant experience or training, when there is a clash of personalities and when you think another practitioner might offer a useful different view, e.g. 'I wonder if it would be helpful for you to see X. She's ...'.

Beginning. See discussion of negotiating a contract. Give the client a chance to compose him/herself, get used to the room and you.

Ending. Say 'In the last few minutes I'd like to ...' or, nearer to the end, 'Is there anything else you want to say to me?'. Try a summary, or ask your interviewee or client to summarise. It is a good idea if possible to have some time to spare between interviews, both to prepare for the next one and because some people leave important information until near the end. A contract helps. Try to end positively (not the same as false optimism): often there will have been some progress in understanding (Stage One of the counselling model), or some agreed action (Stage Three). If verbal signals fail, try non-verbal: sit more upright and, as a last resort, stand up.

Questions which may be embarrassing. Introduce them: 'Some people find this an embarrassing question ...'.

Note-taking. Note-taking need not interfere with the pace and flow of the interview, and need not become more important than listening. Against this, summaries help in remembering the relevant points, and notes can be made immediately after the interview. Compromises are possible, e.g. not taking notes when your interviewee is talking very personally. Obviously, note-taking should not intrude. Interviewees can take notes too, or write out/draw aspects of a problem.

Keeping a record. General issues which need to be considered include: 'Why are records kept?' and 'Who has access to them?' (Bond, 2000). Writing a report – for yourself or others – can help clarify thinking. The stages of the counselling model provide an obvious structure. Part of the value of a structure is that it suggests relevant aspects of people or problems which may have been missed or insufficiently emphasised in the interview. It also encourages questions about the process of interviewing, e.g. 'What stage are we at?', 'Where is it going?', 'What skills did I use?' and 'What other skills might I have used?'. This possibility is more systematically illustrated in the two checklists.

Too talkative. Try summaries and a higher proportion of closed questions. Alternatively, remind your interviewee of the contract, particularly of time. Interrupt: say 'Can we return to ...?'.

Too quiet. There are many reasons for being quiet. Resist the temptation to talk too much yourself. Try the skill of immediacy. Paper-and-pencil techniques can be more gentle. You can ask 'Would it help to sit and think about this for a while?'.

Nervousness. Signs of being nervous – tension, restlessness etc – may indicate something else. Try to find out your interviewee's needs. Answer questions. Ask easy questions first (a good general principle too). Try to keep relaxed yourself, e.g. through breathing slowly and deeply.

Aggression. Take preventive measures (Breakwell, 1997). Try using the person's name. Paraphrase. Overall, show you are trying calmly to understand and want to help. Use assertive skills, e.g. 'I'd like you to stop shouting', 'I'd like to discuss the problem with you'. An aggressive person may be frightened. In any case threats are not likely to be useful: telling someone off sometimes heightens aggression.

Emotional blocking. Indications of emotional blocking – when someone is unaware of an emotion – are abrupt changes of topic and tension. Kennedy-Moore and Watson (1999) recommend very gently saying that the other person seems tense and wondering if it indicates anything (but not pushing for emotional expression) or – if you are trained to do so – using exaggeration or literal description (Bayne *et al.*, 1999). However, interviewers and counsellors sometimes don't notice emotions which are being clearly expressed. They then use such techniques unnecessarily and perhaps unhelpfully.

Client is upset. Try to keep calm yourself. People vary considerably in emotional expressiveness. For example, a useful idea about crying is that there are marked individual differences in peak expression: for one person it's tearful eyes, for another deep sobbing and wailing (Mills and Wooster, 1967). Mills and Wooster recommend helping clients on the verge of crying (a) to cry and (b) to identify their underlying emotions and tensions.

However, it is disrespectful to expect everyone to be emotionally expressive (Kennedy-Moore and Watson, 1999), and sometimes avoiding emotion may be the best way of coping – at least in the short term.

Client is 'flooded'. 'Flooded expression', e.g. when someone cries and cries, or is taken over by any emotion, seems to be unhelpful (Kennedy-Moore and Watson, 1999). This is because it makes thinking and creating meaning impossible. In the model of counselling discussed earlier, emotions are clarified with the right words for the person feeling them. They can then be interpreted, e.g. 'I've felt guilty and ashamed about this for years – but it's not my fault'. Flooding gets in the way.

Techniques to try include deep breathing and distraction. When your interviewee or client is calmer, you might then discuss ways he/she can avoid flooding, and other ways of expressing emotion.

Crisis situation. Essentially, use the three-stage model of counselling but with the emphasis strongly on Stage Three. 'Crisis' means an immediately threatening and highly stressful situation which requires action. The person in crisis is likely to feel overwhelmed, out of control, angry, fearful and despairing. The goal is to restore, as far as possible, the normal level of functioning (Parry, 1990; Bayne *et al.*, 1999; Egan, 2002).

---

putting it into practice

1 When you're listening well, what's going on in your mind? What does 'listening well' mean to you?

2 R.D. Laing wrote, 'It is not so easy for one person to give another a cup of tea' (1969: 106). What did he mean? What are the implications for interviewing and counselling?

3 What current limits to your counselling skills does an analysis using Table 3.3 suggest? When would it be ethical for you to refer a client?

further reading

Feltham, C. and Horton, I. (eds) (2006) *Handbook of Counselling and Psychotherapy*, 2nd edn. London: Sage.

About 60 authors and over a hundred topics with a largely practical emphasis. Balanced, concise and authoritative.

Yalom, I.D. (1989) *Love's Executioner and Other Tales of Psychotherapy*. London: Penguin.

Vivid accounts of counselling with ten clients. Yalom's approach is fairly consistent with the model discussed in this chapter.

4 | Assertiveness and coping with stress

Introduction

Like the interviewing and counselling skills discussed in the previous chapter, assertive skills can improve conversations, meetings, interviews and counselling sessions dramatically. At one level they too can show respect to service users and others. At another level they can contribute to gathering better quality information and to making fair and helpful decisions more often.

However, two cautious notes are important. First, like interviewing and counselling, assertiveness is not just about techniques; it thrives on accurate self-awareness and adequate self-esteem. If you know what you like and dislike, for example, it is easier to say no assertively. Second, assertiveness theory typically emphasises being direct, but some cultural groups value indirectness (Sue and Sue, 1990). 'Bicultural competence' (Rakos, 1991) is a useful notion here. It underlines the principle that using assertiveness skills in a prescriptive way is too simple, and it also respects cultural differences. For example, looking someone straight in the eye is impolite or worse in some cultures, but part of being assertive in others. Bicultural competence treats assertiveness as a widening of the range of options: you can practise saying 'No', for example, both while looking someone in the eye and while looking away.

There is also another way in which assertiveness theory and skills can neglect the social context. For example, suppose you are being harassed at work and you want to be more assertive, e.g. to make a clear request to the person harassing you such as: 'You say that touching me on the shoulder doesn't mean anything, but it matters to me. I would like you to stop doing it'. You can be very pleased with the results of making this request, which is fine as far as it goes. However, it leaves the norms of the organisation intact. One response to this issue is to say that, after considering costs and benefits, you have the option to take it further. Another response is that all techniques and theories have their own field of application and limits, that assertiveness operates at the individual level and other methods are more useful at the level of organisations or cultures. However, actually implementing other methods at these levels may call upon assertive skills.

Assertiveness is a useful technique for coping with stress but also interacts with it. If someone is stressed, it is likely to impede their assertiveness (and their effectiveness generally of course). Therefore this chapter also includes a straightforward model of coping with stress and guidelines on two effective techniques: expressive writing (Smyth, 1998; Bolton *et al.*, 2004) and peer support (Baron and Kerr, 2003). However, although quite a lot is known about which strategies are the most widely used, much less is known about their effectiveness for different people and different sources of stress.

Assertive skills

Assertiveness can be defined as 'expressing and acting on your rights as a person, while respecting the rights of other people'.

Assertiveness theory and skills can be applied with varying degrees of formality, ranging from a thorough, systematic analysis of situations and 'skills deficits' in a standard behavioural approach to a discussion of possible ways of feeling and behaving differently in a more 'humanistic' one. Rakos (1991) calls the more formal approach 'assertiveness *therapy*' and the less formal 'assertiveness *training*'. In either therapy or training, role play with coaching can be helpful, and some consideration of likely costs and benefits is very desirable before trying out the new skill in a real situation. 'Coaching' may sound as if there is one right way to be assertive. On the contrary, good coaching values individuality, authenticity and spontaneity, not a mechanical, polished but lifeless performance.

In the rest of this section, the basic elements of several assertive skills and their refinements are outlined. I have drawn mainly on Anne Dickson's (1982) book, *A Woman in Your Own Right*, the best practical book on assertiveness, for men too. Dickson also discusses arguments for and against using each skill, e.g. we sometimes don't ask for what we'd like (make a request) because we:

- put others first, 'It's not that important'.
- are afraid of rejection.
- don't want to impose; one or both of you might be embarrassed.
- expect the other person, especially if she/he cares for you, to know without being asked: 'I shouldn't have to ask.'
- don't want to feel obliged to the other person.

On the other hand, there are consequences of *not* making requests:

- Frustration: small irritations may build up until you 'explode' or you may express your frustration indirectly, e.g. by nagging, sulking, complaining to others, being a 'martyr'.
- You may lose touch with what you do want.

The general choice everyone makes is whether the results of not asking for something are worse or better for them than those of asking and being refused. Being clear about your rights and the rights of other people can be very helpful in making such choices. Table 4.1 (overleaf) lists a fairly representative set of assertive rights in its lefthand column. The format, taken from Bond (1986), makes explicit the 'respect for others' element in being assertive.

You may like to consider the righthand column first. How easy or difficult do you find each to accept as a right for other people? Then compare your reactions to the lefthand column. Are there any rights in either column that you want to cross out? Any to add? It can be helpful, when you are upset or angry in a way that seems out of proportion, to take each right in turn and see if you are respecting it or not.

Making requests

The skill of making requests contrasts with paraphrasing: it is putting yourself to the fore rather than trying to see from another person's point of view. In everyday life the two skills are complementary. Rogers (1975), at the level of personal qualities, argued for more empathy in relationships generally, but in everyday life for genuineness above all, i.e. stating wants, intentions and feelings.

The basic elements of making a request are:

1. Choose person and request carefully. Consider the possible costs and benefits, your values and your rights (Table 4.1).
2. Write out the request; make sure it is brief, specific (concrete), and does not sabotage itself by implying either that they must agree or

Table 4.1 Assertive rights

1	I have the right to be treated with respect.	*and*	Others have the right to be treated with respect.
2	I have the right to express my thoughts, opinions and values.	*and*	Others have the right to express their thoughts, opinions and values.
3	I have the right to express my feelings.	*and*	Others have the right to express their feelings.
4	I have the right to say 'No' without feeling guilty.	*and*	Others have the right to say 'No' without feeling guilty.
5	I have the right to be successful.	*and*	Others have the right to be successful.
6	I have the right to make mistakes.	*and*	Others have the right to make mistakes.
7	I have the right to change my mind.	*and*	Others have the right to change their minds.
8	I have the right to say that I don't understand.	*and*	Others have the right to say that they don't understand.
9	I have the right to ask for what I want.	*and*	Others have the right to ask for what they want.
10	I have the right to decide for myself whether or not I am responsible for another person's problem.	*and*	Others have the right to decide for themselves whether or not they are responsible for another person's problem.
11	I have the right to choose not to assert myself.	*and*	Others have the right to choose not to assert themselves.

that you expect them to say no. Try to assume that you don't know the answer. The request can be either for someone to do something, e.g. go for a drink, or to stop doing something, e.g. playing music too loudly for you. Dickson (1982) gives numerous excellent examples.

3. Rehearse (real or imaginary), with feedback from yourself and, ideally, from skilful observers. Rehearsal and coaching might also take into account possible reactions to a range of replies, setting aside a time for constructive analysis of the outcome, and deciding when and where to make the request. Contingency plans appeal to some people. Overall, the idea is to use assertiveness theory and methods flexibly and creatively and in a way that suits you.

4. Review the refinements in the next paragraph and consider their relevance to this request.

5. Rehearse again. Observe in particular *how* you ask. Slight adjustments to the way you stand, hold your shoulders, or expression, will make you look – and probably feel – more assertive.

6. Select time and place to actually make the request.

7. Try it.

8. Consider the outcome, using the principles of giving feedback outlined in Chapter 3 on interviewing and counselling.

Refinements of the skill are:

1. When asking someone to stop doing something, or to do something she/he does not want to do, *calm repetition* can be a key element. The request tends to become easier to say as you repeat it, and to be said more definitely, as long as it is what you genuinely want.

2. Repetition is also a way (perhaps combined with paraphrasing) of responding to protests and irrelevant logic. Essentially, the idea is to say 'Yes I realise you are disappointed, but I would like ...', and so on.

3. You may also like to suggest consequences (perhaps best held in reserve), or to combine your request with a compliment, itself an assertive skill and therefore with risks and benefits to be taken into account.

The other main skills are outlined next.

Saying no

Basic skill:
- be brief
- speak clearly and confidently (watch for inappropriate smiles and apologies).

Refinements:
- notice your first reaction (to take it into account, not necessarily to act on it)
- if unsure, ask for time and/or further details
- calm repetition may be useful (cf. Dickson's image of a swaying tree)
- offer an alternative?
- empathy?
- put in context?

Giving compliments

Basic skill:
- be specific (about the effect on you and/or what it is you like).

Refinements:
- do not use when making a request!

Receiving compliments

Basic skill:
- thank the person straightforwardly
- enjoy the compliment (if it pleases you).

Refinements:
- consider basic skill *plus* asking for detail
- consider basic skill *plus* saying what you think
- avoid complimenting him/her back too quickly.

Giving criticism

Basic skill:
- be specific about what it is the other person is doing, and about what you would like him/her to do that would be different (c.f. the skill of making requests)
- be specific about effects on you
- take one thing at a time
- avoid labels like 'selfish' and 'lazy'.

Refinements:
- listen to the other person's reaction (you may have misinter-preted his/her behaviour, he/she may have misunderstood your constructive intent)
- be specific about the consequences, (a) if the other person changes, and/or (b) if she/he does not
- put in context.

Receiving criticism

The main perspective is that, even from someone you have little or no time for, criticism may contain useful information. Also, using the skill well breaks a normal pattern of interaction and illustrates the assertive right that making mistakes is normal and human.

Basic skill:
- consider thanking her/him and agreeing with all or part of the comments
- consider saying what you will do differently next time (if appropriate), or that you'll think about how to improve whatever was wrong.

Refinements:
If you disagree with all or part of the criticism, consider one or more of:
- thanking him/her
- asking for examples or details
- saying 'I don't agree'
- paraphrasing.

Coping with stress

It can be argued that it is professionally responsible for anyone whose work involves caring for others to take care of themselves too, both physically and psychologically, partly because you are then more likely to work well. It is easy to believe this but still get 'caught up' or 'sucked in' – vivid metaphors. There are usually far more people to see and things to do than anyone could possibly manage.

This section first discusses stress and coping briefly, and then outlines two coping strategies: expressive writing and being in a peer support group.

There are numerous definitions of stress. Bond's (1986) definition is 'the experience of unpleasant over or under stimulation as defined by the individual in question, that actually or potentially leads to ill health' (p. 2). This definition emphasises individual experience, and hints at feeling threatened and strained to the extent of being overwhelmed. Cooper *et al.* (2001: 2–14) and Jones and Bright (2001: 6–7) discuss other definitions but I don't think any of them improve on Bond's.

There are many problematic aspects of stress apart from definition: the relative importance of external and internal factors in causing it, whether it is more effective to intervene at the level of organisational and social structures or at the level of individuals, motives for *not* looking after yourself, which ways of coping with stress are most effective for which kinds of problems and/or people, how important stress is in various illnesses and, when it is important in illness, the processes involved (Sapolsky, 1998; Cooper *et al.*, 2001; Jones and Bright, 2001).

A three-stage model for coping with stress is:

Stage 1 Monitor signs of too much or too little stimulation, especially *early* warnings
Stage 2 Choose one or more coping strategies
Stage 3 Try them out, monitoring the effects.

Table 4.2 lists a few of the more common effects or signs of stress. It is important to note that some of these may be caused by *illness* rather than stress, and may therefore need medical attention.

Table 4.2   Some effects of stress

On thoughts and emotions	On the body	On behaviour
– difficulty concentrating	– tight throat	– irritability
	– sweating	– accidents
– anxiety	– dry mouth	– drugs
– tiredness	– tics	– being critical
– boredom	– frequent urination	– difficulties in sleeping
– depression	– aches	

Expressive writing

The key researcher in this area is James Pennebaker. For example, Pennebaker *et al.* (1990) divided students who had just started their first year into two random groups. The experimental group were asked to write for 20 minutes on three consecutive days about their 'very deepest thoughts and feelings about coming to college'. The control or comparison group wrote on what they'd done since they woke up that day. Therefore, thoughts and feelings were emphasised in the first group, and behaviour in the second.

The main finding was that students in the experimental group went to the health centre less in the next six months than those in the control group. The basic finding and variations have been replicated several times, with some attention to explaining the positive effects of this form of writing on health (Smyth, 1998). For example, in Spera *et al.* (1994), unemployed professionals either wrote about their reactions to redundancy (experimental group) or to relatively superficial matters (control group). Those in the experimental group found new jobs more quickly but *not* because they applied for more jobs or wrote more letters. For excellent critical reviews of the research and applications, see Smyth (1998) and Kennedy-Moore and Watson (1999).

A model of coping consistent with Pennebaker's research and with the model of counselling discussed earlier is outlined below with an example. A key principle is to take both inner experience and action seriously.

Model and example

Step 1: Reflection

Write as *freely* as you can about something that matters to you – not analysing, not concerned with literary merit, and for yourself only.

> *Longer run than usual on Monday. In the night pain in my knee woke me up, and yesterday it was stiff and I hobbled. Felt despairing and angry: I'll have to stop running. Also annoyed that I'd just bought new running shoes, and disturbed by the strength of my reaction. I was flat and ill most of the day at work, and abrupt with some of my colleagues. During the day my knee eased. This morning it's near normal. Feel much more buoyant and constructive.*

End of step 1 – reflection – at least on this occasion.

Step 2: Analysis

Analyse your reactions and perhaps challenge them, for example:

- Be specific
- What is the evidence for any assertions and beliefs?
- Is there a familiar feeling or pattern there?
- What assumptions are you making?
- Does your reaction tell you anything else about yourself, e.g. suggest important values?
- How realistic are you being?
- What other ways (however unlikely) are there of looking at what happened?

I'm left wondering about my reaction to injury (and illness).
1 I believe it's awful and catastrophic not to be able to run.
2 It's a recurring pattern. It may be related to lots of illness as a child, especially being scared I'd stop breathing.
3 Everyone is ill or injured sometimes (especially good athletes!). It's normal.

End of Step 2 – a more considered analysis. It is meant to contrast with Step 1 which is written more freely, indeed as freely as possible.

Step 3: Action

Consider possible actions.

- Is there any action you want to take now?
- Is there anything which you might do differently next time?

Possible actions:
1 Look up knee injuries. Preventive measures?
2 Ask Dave's advice.
3 Make a special effort re 'flatness' next time: perhaps explain to other people, 'go into' my feelings, treat it like loss. Do 1 and 2 today.

Evaluation of the example

Analysis is relatively neglected but a useful start is made. The actions are relevant and promising, but could be expressed more specifically.

Other writing techniques include making lists, e.g. of things you're happy about, wants, problems; freewriting; writing about yourself in the third person; and writing dialogues between part of you and another part of you, or with another person (Rainer, 1978; Bolton *et al.*, 2004).

Peer support groups

A peer support group usually consists of people in the same general situation who agree to offer support and challenge to each other. The skills outlined in the chapter on interviewing and counselling are useful. If an overall aim and strategy are agreed, then anything that happens in the group can be evaluated on whether it is consistent with the aims and strategy or not, e.g. the amount of time any one person in the group speaks, whether to allow silent members or not, whether to practise new behaviours or not, when to allow new members, and so on. One way of using expressive writing is to share extracts with another person, a supervisor or a support group (Murray, 1998).

It's not clear what social support is or how it protects (Baron and Kerr, 2003), but it is powerful. For example, in one study, conversation with an allocated untrained person halved the length of labour in childbirth. Explanations currently include perceived control, increased self-esteem and self-disclosure (as in expressive writing). Sense of belonging and involvement is another possibility. On the other hand, groups can also be undermining. For example, Newsom (1999) found that social 'support' can lead to feelings of incompetence and guilt. Relevant behaviour may include being critical (rather than skilfully challenging) and being condescending (Baron and Kerr, 2003).

Some suggestions for running a support group are:

● for each member of the group to have equal time;
● to negotiate the amount of structure – some effective groups are highly structured but others are free-wheeling;
● no discussion of any aspect of the group (process or content) outside the group;
● the person speaking asks for the kind of support they'd like, e.g. basic listening, empathy, challenging, sharing factual information, advice, encouragement (Bond, 1986);
● review your group after some meetings (or all of them): What is working well? What could work better?;
● look out for 'games', e.g. 'Ain't it awful', in which the group reinforce each other's sense of gloom and powerlessness;

'Psychologist'; and the three roles in the Drama Triangle: Victim, Persecutor and Rescuer (Bayne *et al.*, 1999);

● notice and challenge any interfering beliefs about asking for or accepting support, make a note of them and challenge them. Examples of interfering beliefs are:

- I don't have time
- It's not fair on other people
- I'm not worth it
- It shows I can't cope
- Other people aren't interested
- Other people don't care
- I can cope on my own
- It may make me vulnerable.

Generally, these beliefs are unhelpful, and, for social workers and other practitioners in the helping professions, inconsistent and disrespectful of self and others.

putting it into practice

1 How assertive do you think you are? Try listing occasions on which you (a) wanted to say no but didn't, (b) wanted to ask someone for something but didn't. Taking into account the generally accepted view in the literature on assertiveness that no one should be assertive, or could be assertive, all the time, what are the implications of these occasions for improving your skills?

2 How do you relax?

3 Research and evaluate the evidence on the effectiveness of your favourite method of coping with stress.

Further reading

Bond, M. (1986) *Stress and Self-awareness. A Guide for Nurses.* London: Heinemann.

Notable for its non-patronising tone and for its thoughtful discussions of 'pitfalls' in using various strategies for coping with stress. A new edition would be very welcome (15 + years is a long time in this area) but I think it is the best practical book on coping with stress, and just as relevant to social workers as it is to nurses.

Dickson, A. (1982) *A Woman in Your Own Right*. London: Quartet.

The best practical book on assertivess – for men too. Considers arguments for and against each assertive skill with excellent guidelines and examples.

Jones, F. and Bright, G. (2001) *Stress. Myth, Theory and Research*. London: Prentice Hall.

Sophisticated and clear review of ideas and research, in five sections: What is stress?, What effects stress might have, Why do people react differently to stressors?, A focus on stress at work, and Stress reduction strategies.

5 | Psychological type and communication

Introduction

Social workers frequently need to understand other people's personalities and motives, to predict their behaviour and to communicate effectively. This chapter outlines a widely used personality theory and applies it to communication problems and strategies. This is psychological type theory in the Myers-Briggs Type Indicator (MBTI) sense (Myers with Myers, 1980; Bayne, 2004), and it has several strengths. First, the evidence for its validity is at least as strong as it is for rival theories, especially the strong relationship between MBTI results and scores on measures of four of the Big Five personality characteristics (Bayne, 2005): Big Five theory has dominated mainstream personality research for many years, much as MBTI theory has dominated applied personality theory. Second, it is a very positive and constructive theory. Third, it is useful at the straightforward level discussed here but has deeper levels too.

The chapter is in three main parts:

1. An outline of psychological type or MBTI theory, emphasising the central concept of preference and touching on the main motives of each type. Often the most effective way of communicating with someone, including empathising with and influencing her/him, is to understand his/her main motive or goal. The preferences, and indirectly the motives, of each psychological type are illustrated in three areas of life relevant to many social workers and service users: choice of career (or, more broadly, occupation/activity), learning styles, and dealing with money.
2. Psychological type theory is then applied directly to communication problems and strategies.
3. The theory is useful at two general levels of understanding: that people differ so profoundly and the nature of those differences.

However, it is most effectively applied when accurate judgements of type are made. This section of the chapter outlines current knowledge about improving the accuracy of judgements of type and other personal qualities.

Psychological type theory

The theory's general aims are: (1) to help people understand and respect themselves, and (2) to help us understand and respect others. There is a major emphasis on the 'constructive use of differences', as opposed to judging people of different types to ourselves to be stupid, inefficient, awkward or mad. More specific applications include team-building, leadership training, career development and relationship counselling.

The concept of 'preference'

In type theory, preference is used to mean 'feeling most natural and comfortable with a particular way of behaving and experiencing'. For example, someone with a preference for Introversion will, given normal type development and the opportunities, behave introvertedly most of the time and extravertedly some of the time, and Introversion will feel more comfortable and natural to them. For someone with a preference for Extraversion the opposite is the case.

The concept of preference has two valuable and contrasting qualities: it provides stability, coherence and continuity to personality and at the same time recognises some degree of flexibility. Such flexibility could be vacuous, appearing to explain behaviour but not predicting it. Psychological type theory is more subtle: it states that most people most of the time behave in ways that are consistent with their preferences and thus can be understood and predicted to a useful extent (Bayne, 2005).

The theory is sometimes criticised for putting people in boxes, for being too rigid and too simple. The concept of preference is one argument against this criticism. Another is the model of development in the theory, which is optimistic about how much we tend to develop our preferences because it assumes that most people's early experience encourages, or at least does not greatly discourage, their development (K. Myers and Kirby, 1994; Bayne, 2004, 2005). 'Development' here means trusting and using each preference more than its opposite, as in the example of Extraversion–Introversion earlier, but also developing the opposite, though to a lesser extent. This is seen as happening throughout a person's life (K. Myers and Kirby, 1994).

The four pairs of preferences and sixteen types

This section allows you to choose your own type if you wish. If so, please choose in a *provisional* way, behaving like a good detective (Carr, 1997). Your aim is to isolate your basic enduring preferences from other influences on your behaviour. The 'other influences' include culture, upbringing, roles, other personality characteristics, stress, self-image (e.g. as ideal woman, man or social worker) and type development, hence the need to gather clues and interpret them carefully. This may sound a formidable task but it is generally achievable.

Geneally the most effective way of discovering one's psychological type is through the MBTI questionnaire itself plus skilful feedback. However, there are many other ways of clarifying preferences and types, including reading descriptions of the types (e.g. in *Introduction to Type*, I. Myers with Kirby and K. Myers, 1998); asking someone who knows you well to read your choice of the closest descriptions; and observing your comfort with and energy for different ways of behaving (Carr, 1997; Bayne, 2004, 2005). MBTI results are themselves still only a clue, as the term 'Indicator' implies, though generally the best clue.

There are four pairs of preferences:

Extraversion	(E)	or	Introversion	(I)
Sensing	(S)	or	Intuition	(N)
Thinking	(T)	or	Feeling	(F)
Judging	(J)	or	Perceiving	(P)

The meaning of each preference is indicated in Table 5.1 but please note that their names have a particular, technical meaning in this theory, that, for example, Thinking does *not* mean 'without feelings' and Judging does *not* mean 'judgmental'.

A person's psychological type is one of each of the four pairs of preferences e.g. ISTP or ENTP. There are sixteen combinations and therefore sixteen types. However, I have come across a few people who seemed, both to themselves and to me, equally comfortable with both preferences in a pair and who therefore described themselves as,

Table 5.1	Characteristics associated with each preference		
E	More outgoing and active	More reflective and reserved	I
S	More practical and interested in facts and details	More interested in possibilities and an overview	N
T	More logical and reasoned	More agreeable and appreciative	F
J	More planning and coming to conclusions	More easy-going and flexible	P

say, EFP or IST. Whether they are best described as two types or one type with excellent development of a non-preference is arguable (Bayne, 2005) and doesn't reduce the practical value of the theory. Indeed, each pair of preferences can be very useful on its own, as is shown in a later section of this chapter (pp. 97–100).

Types and motives

In MBTI theory the term 'type' is a statement about personality structure. The central idea is that in each person one of the four preferences for S, N, T or F is dominant – the managing director of the personality – another second, and so on. The characteristics associated with a person's dominant preference, given sufficiently normal development, are the main elements of their personality. It 'dominates and unifies their life' (Myers with Myers, 1980: 10).

In terms of motives, K. Myers and Kirby (1994) suggest the following goals for each dominant function (extracted from pp. 12–14):

S (+EP) to experience as much as possible; to have an unending variety of sensing experience.

S (+IJ) to form a sold, substantial, and accurate understanding of the world around them and their place in it.

N (+EP) to find and explore new possibilities, new and exciting challenges.

N (+IJ) to develop their inner intuitive patterns for understanding the world.

T (+EF) to create logical order in their external world, make their environment rational.

T (+IP) to create logical order internally, to develop rational principles for understanding the world.

F (+EJ) to create harmony and cooperation in their external environment, to facilitate others in getting what they need and want.

F (+IP) to develop their internal core of values, establish an external life that is congruent with them, and help both individuals and humankind fulfil their potential.

Type and careers

There are strong relationships between type and choice of career but the theory recognises that minority types in a particular career can contribute to it in unusual and positive ways. They can also find and create niches, which implies that studies of job satisfaction need to focus on the appeal of different aspects of a job to different types as well as on the appeal of the whole job (Myers *et al.*, 1998; Bayne, 2004).

There are as yet no studies of type and social workers. The nearest may be Dodd and Bayne (in press) on counsellors. They found, for exmple, that Ts tended to choose cognitive models of counselling and Fs affective ones and that choice of cognitive behaviour therapy (CBT) was related to preferences for S and J, choice of the psychodynamic model to INFJ, and choice of psychosynthesis to INFP.

These relationships are consistent with MBTI theory. However, there are many exceptions. For example, other types are also drawn to CBT, though less often and probably for different reasons. NTs, for example, may be enjoying the rich variations in dysfunctional beliefs and challenging their logic.

Overall, the relationships between type and choice of counselling model definitely do *not* mean that a person of the 'wrong' type for a model (or career) should avoid it, rather that they should examine their motives with particular care and be prepared for most of their colleagues to be of different types from themselves. The same principle applies to choice of social work and specialism or niche within it. Tieger and Barron-Tieger (2001) suggest motives for career satisfaction for each type, as well as characteristic strategies and potential pitfalls in actually searching for a fulfilling career. Bayne (2004) applies type theory to job descriptions, application forms and selection interviews.

Because psychological type (MBTI) theory is a general theory it has many applications. Apart from those already touched on, they include child-rearing, education, coping with procrastination, health, coping with stress, and leading and managing.

Type and learning styles

Aspects of the learning styles associated with each preference are listed in Table 5.2 (cf. DiTiberio and Hammer, 1993; Lawrence, 1997). They vary dramatically. For example, brainstorming is as natural as breathing for some types, but pointless and threatening to others. Similarly, a student's preferred learning style or styles will inevitably match the teaching styles of some tutors and clash with others. This is most likely to cause trouble and injustice when tutors are not aware of their own biases.

The biases can be very persistent. For example, Smith (1993) compared the comments on an essay made by six lecturers with a preference for Thinking (T) and six with a preference for Feeling (F). All the lecturers were experienced teachers of English. They all put comments in the margins of the essay and summarised strengths and weaknesses (or 'areas to develop') at the end. They all also agreed on the mark for the essay, wrote about the same amount of feedback and used similar numbers of questions and reactions. However, the differences were striking too, especially as their department had explicit guidelines on giving feedback on essays: the F lecturers praised the essay twice as much as the Ts and wrote twice as many suggestions.

Table 5.2 The preference and aspects of learning style
E action, talk, trial and error
I reflection, private work
S close observation of what actually happens; starts with the concrete and specific, ideas and theory later
N theory first; links and possibilities; surges of interest
T analysis and logic; critiques
F harmonious atmosphere; need to care about the topic
J more formal; organised; clear expectations and criteria
P flexible; not routine; bursts of energy; work as play

Smith suggested that these striking differences illustrate different philosophies of teaching associated with preferences for T and F. The suggested T philosophy is that students do (or should) focus on their weaknesses, on 'what is the problem that needs solving?' (p. 40). In contrast, the F philosophy is to encourage students to develop their strengths first. Smith found greater concern on the part of the F lecturers about students' feelings and greater emphasis on the part of the T lecturers on essay content and potential learning. An obvious practical question is the impact of the different styles of feedback on students generally, and on T and F students respectively, but students' views on the two approaches to giving feedback haven't been studied yet.

Another example of a marked difference in approach to an aspect of studying is the reactions of people to deadlines. People with a preference for Judging (J) tend to start a piece of work early and, circumstances allowing, finish it well before the deadline. Their motives, according to theory, are enjoyment of closure and avoiding what they experience as the stress of an imminent deadline. (About 10 per cent of Js are exceptions: Quenk *et al.*, 2001.) Conversely, people with a preference for Perceiving (P) tend to do their best work at the last minute; they like to keep things open and they enjoy an imminent-deadline energy surge. (About 40 per cent of Ps are exceptions: Quenk *et al.*, 2001.) Js and Ps produce equally good work, but in their contrasting styles and with characteristic strengths and weaknesses (Table 5.2).

Type development can compensate for these weaknesses. For example, Js tend to be more skilled than Ps at writing conclusions to essays and lab reports, and Ps at integrating more diverse material, but just as Js can learn to return to a 'finished' essay and add another idea or more notes of caution, so Ps can learn to add a careful conclusion.

Type and money

Type theory assumes that each type has a natural approach to money, derived from core motives. Knowing your own approach can help you to use it and to advise others more effectively, probably by moderating their approach and supplementing it with aspects of the approaches of other types. Taking a simple level of the theory, SPs (a combination of Sensing and Perceiving) tend to spend money to feel free and excited; SJs tend to be careful with money, to try to achieve security and stability; NTs try to spend it perfectly (competence is their core motive); and NFs tend to ignore it (because their core motive of self-actualisation is rather more vague and not materialistic).

In the theory each of these approaches is valid and has strengths (Linder, 2000). However, the strengths can be taken too far and they can also be modified as part of type development. For example, an SP might achieve more excitement from other sources than spending money and, through developing their Judging 'side', might save. Similarly, NTs, especially INTPs, might set a time limit on their detailed comparative analyses of a particular purchase, and develop their ability to make decisions in a Feeling way to supplement (not replace or equal) their Thinking decisions (Bayne, 2004).

Communication problems and strategies

Psychological type theory suggests the conflicts which are most likely between people with different preferences (Table 5.3) and some strategies for trying to resolve them (Table 5.4).

Examples of the main reactions and prejudices, according to MBTI theory, are that Introverts may feel overwhelmed, hurried, or invaded by Extraverts, and Es may see Is as dull and slow; Sensing types may be seen as boring by those with a preference for Intuition, and Ns as grandiose by Ss; Thinking types as being obsessed with reasons and unsympathetic by Feeling types, and Fs as lacking any logic and too soft by Ts; Judging types as pushy and rigid by Perceiving types, and Ps as aimless and disorganised by Js.

Table 5.3   Some communication problems between people with opposite preferences

Between E and I:	need to talk v. need to be alone
Between S and N:	focus on details and realism v. focus on general picture, links and speculation
Between T and F:	being seen as unsympathetic and critical v. being seen as illogical and too agreeable
Between J and P:	controlling and planning v. flexible and very open to change

Table 5.4 Some strategies for managing and preventing communication problems between people with opposite preferences.

E with I	Allow time for privacy and to reflect.	
I with E	Explain need for time alone, allow for the other person's need to talk in order to clarify.	
S with N	Overall picture first, with relevant details later.	
N with S	Say a particular idea is half-formed and/or include relevant detail.	
T with F	Include effects on people, begin with points of agreement.	
F with T	Include reasons and consequences, be brief.	
J with P	Allow for some flexibility in plans, style of working, etc. and for the other's need not to be controlled.	
P with J	Allow for some planning and structure and for the other person's need to control and decide.	

These potential problems follow straightforwardly from the theory. Let's take a more specific example: a social worker with a preference for Feeling and a service user with a preference for Thinking. The social worker sees the service user as distant and impersonal and feels rebuffed and silly. If he applies type theory, he will first accept that the service user (whether actually having a preference for Thinking or just behaving like it at the time) does not want to be friendly at this time. He therefore changes his own manner accordingly. In a sense, he switches to the other person's 'language' (in this case Thinking) while being ready to switch again if he thinks it appropriate. He then does not feel so rebuffed, even though people with a preference for Feeling tend to be more sensitive to perceived criticism and to need harmony more than those who prefer Thinking. Rather, he feels empathic and skilful and the service user feels more understood and more respectfully treated.

The four 'languages' distinguished by Susan Brock in the most widely used approach to type and communication (e.g. Allen and Brock, 2000) are ST, SF, NT and NF:

ST   brief and concise, emphasises facts and logic, does not go
        off at tangents, and starts at the beginning.
SF   same practical flavour as ST but warmer, friendlier, more
        personal.
NF   personal and general, interested in possiblities with details
        to be worked out later.
NT   same general flavour as NF but emphasises reasoning and
        competence more, is calm and objective.

These four languages affect the content and tone of communications
while E and I affect the pace, and J and P the tendency to move
towards closure (J) or keep things open (P).

The theory also offers an explanation for strong mutual attraction
of opposites, when for example Js are attracted to Ps' easy-going
flexibility and Ps to Js' order: each person has what the other
(relatively) lacks. They may then – especially if they don't know type
theory – attempt to change each other to be more like themselves. The
theory predicts that these attempts will fail.

Good communication is much more than knowing one's preferences and matching 'language', but applying type theory does make it
more likely. The following example illustrates this point. An ENFP
counsellor was counselling an ISFJ client (Provost, 1993). The client
was depressed. She saw herself as a slow learner, was impatient with
complexity, and described her life as 'dull and devoid of fun'. Provost,
an ENFP, controlled her natural, relatively bold approach: 'Our
relationship was a series of gentle pushes, cautious tries, and
sometimes retreats' (p. 52). She suspects that if she had tried to work
at her own pace rather than her client's, the client would have clung
to the familiar ways or left. Occasionally, Provost tried a paradoxical
suggestion: 'You're not ready to change – let's be more cautious.' She
also helped this client appreciate her (the client's) strengths, for
example, organisation (developed J) and warmth and caring
(developed F), and they agreed on some specific goals, for example,
to try out some additional learning strategies and to become more
playful and flexible. Provost adds that she learned to be more patient
from this client, and that 'mutual respect and fascination with each
other's processes were important elements in our counseling relationship' (p. 52).

Other good sources on type theory and communication are Allen
and Brock (2000), Tieger and Barron-Tieger (2001), Dunning (2003)

and VanSant (2003). Paul Tieger and Barbara Barron-Tieger discuss all combinations of the types in romantic relationships but much of what they say applies to work and other relationships too.

Observing type (and other qualities) more accurately

The general 'spirit' of type theory is probably in itself a positive influence on communicating, but accurate observation of the psychological type of those involved is also desirable. There are a number of obstacles to accuracy and some strategies to counteract them. However, people's observations of personality are often quite accurate (Kenrick and Funder, 1988; Funder, 1995, 2001) so it's a matter of improvement rather than major change. At the same time, the serious impact of many of the decisions made by social workers makes even small improvements in accuracy worthwhile.

The obstacles include the nature of perception, the disproportionate power of stereotypes, first impressions, similarity and the ambiguity of non-verbal communication. The process of seeing, for example, includes upside-down images on our eyes and this information passing to the brain in the form of electrical impulses. When people have worn special glasses which invert the images – in a sense put them the right way up – they have adapted to the glasses in about a week, seeing things through them as they normally do (Kosslyn and Rosenberg, 2004). This phenomenon also illustrates what has been called the 'effort after meaning', which we habitually make to the extent of seeing meaning where there is very unlikely to be any. Perception seems like taking a series of photographs but is more like making a sketch or a cartoon. Selection is inevitable but it may mean missing crucial bits of information. It also makes prejudice possible.

Stereotypes are the extreme misuse of categories: a person is judged on the basis of one quality, e.g. age, sex, culture or occupation, when people of, for instance, the same culture vary considerably in personality (Myers et al., 1998). One stereotype that appears to be generally believed is that 'what is beautiful is good' (Baron and Byrne, 2004). It appears at an early age: even nursery school children tend to prefer their more beautiful peers. Similarly, people have been asked to judge reports of 'rather severe' classroom disturbances, apparently described by a teacher. Photographs of the child who caused the trouble were attached to the reports. The judges all saw the same reports but the photograph, of a physically attractive or unattractive child, varied. The effect was a tendency to place more blame on unattractive children – 'a real problem' – than attractive children – 'a bad day ... her cruelty ... need not be taken too seriously'. Such results are obviously unjust – but a human tendency which can be counteracted.

Impressions tend to be formed very quickly and almost automatically (Baron and Byrne, 2004). Just a name sometimes suggests a certain kind of person: expecting something from all people called Judith, for example, because of one Judith in your life. Allport (1961) suggested that if you merely glance at strangers and then let yourself imagine what they are like, a wealth of associations will probably appear. This is probably more true of some psychological types than others.

We also tend to pay most attention to our first impressions, treating them as revealing the 'real person' and tending to see later, discrepant information as unrepresentative: 'Bipasha is very friendly normally, she was tired today', because she was friendly the first time we met her, or in the first few minutes of the first meeting. This effect (called the primacy effect) is easy to counteract, with a simple warning being enough for most people. However, there may then be a recency effect, which can be just as misleading.

The most direct way of countering the disproportionate power of first impressions is to notice them, to check the evidence on which they are based, and to look for further evidence. Less obviously, look for evidence supporting the *opposite* hypothesis too (Lord *et al.*, 1984). A further strategy is to think of alternative interpretations of the evidence.

These strategies all involve suspending belief in one's first impressions until sufficient information has been gathered. How much is 'sufficient'? It depends, but Epstein's research (e.g. 1979) suggests finding three supporting pieces of evidence before accepting a particular judgement. The supervisor at a holiday camp who judged me as a 'surprisingly good worker for a student' on the basis of a surprise visit in which she found me polishing vigorously, would have been more accurate if she had tried two more surprise visits, had observed me working in other situations, and had considered alternative interpretations of her single observation, e.g. novelty of the task, energetic mood.

Strong liking or disliking at first meeting is particularly likely to be an inaccurate and unjust reaction, based on reacting to the person as if they are somebody else. The following six steps are developed from co-counselling (e.g. Evison and Horobin, 2006). In co-counselling, or at least one approach to it, the steps are carried out openly in the relationship. In other situations they will generally be carried out privately, at the time or later.

1. Ask 'Who does this person remind me of?'.
2. In what way is she/he (the new person) like X? Find as many specific similarities as possible, e.g. 'the way he holds his head'.
3. What do I want to say to X?
4. Say it.
5. In what ways is the new person (Y) not like X? Again, look for specific differences.
6. Say 'This is Y, not X'.

The idea, of course, is to see the new person more clearly. It is also possible to suggest that this kind of confusion may be happening to a client who is reacting very strongly to you, and then, if appropriate, to take them through the six steps.

Both small and large similarities tend to be attractive in another person, e.g. their choice of newspaper, speed of thought, sense of humour. This may be because it feels good to have our views confirmed, because we anticipate that if someone agrees with us they are more likely to like us, because we feel more likely to be understood, etc. For accuracy of judgement, it means simply to beware of the 'like me' bias – of immediate positive judgements based on similarity.

Interpreting non-verbal communication

Useful information can be observed and conveyed non-verbally, especially as non-verbal communication (NVC) tends to operate outside or on the fringe of consciousness and is therefore more difficult to fake than words. It is the likely basis of many first impressions: 'There was something about her', 'It was just a feeling'. It gives human communication great versatility but makes misinterpretations more likely (Brems, 2001). The influence of culture on NVCs adds considerably to this potential for error (Sue and Sue, 1990).

'Channels' of NVC can be categorised as follows:

1. The way we use space, including touch (technically known as proxemics).
2. Movements, gestures and expressions (kinesics).
3. More static aspects of the body and surroundings.
4. Aspects of speech other than words: tone, loudness, pauses, etc. (paralanguage).

1. *Use of space*. How close people like to be physically to others varies; it matters who the other person is and what the situation is, but there are also consistent general preferences, and class, sex and race differences in these. For example, people from South America, Arab countries and Pakistan stand closest, those from the UK, USA and Sweden farthest. This is not a trivial matter: it can lead to misunderstandings, with a kind of dance taking place, the pursuing person interpreting the other's behaviour as cold and unfriendly, the pursued person finding the other too 'pushy'.

Seating arrangements may also matter. It has been suggested, for example, that chairs placed across the corner of a desk are generally preferred to chairs across a desk or without a desk. Touch is a closely related NVC; again some marked cultural differences have been found. With a particular person, a pat on the arm may be a powerful way of making contact – especially if you do it 'naturally' – or it may be strongly resented as patronising or intrusive. It may also be very unhelpful, e.g. touching someone to stop them crying because *you* feel uncomfortable.

2. *Gestures, etc.* There are many intriguing ideas about gestures (broadly defined), e.g. are flared nostrils and tight lips signs of tension and fear? One of the most studied NVCs in this category is eye-contact, which is used in part to help regulate conversations. In the UK the usual pattern is that one person talks and sometimes looks directly at the person who is listening, while the person listening looks at the person talking most of the time, until it is their turn to speak. Occasionally, two people's ways of indicating 'I want to speak' or 'It's your turn' take time to mesh, or fail completely. Eye-contact may also indicate interest or hostility, depending on cultural and other factors and in some cultures *lack* of eye-contact indicates interest (Sue and Sue, 1990). Numerous gestures have also been proposed as clues to psychological type, but have not been tested yet (Bayne, 2005).

3. *Static aspects of NVC*. These include clothing, physique, even offices and buildings: what do your surroundings 'say' to your service users? On clothes, physique and characteristics like bowed lips and wearing glasses, there is some agreement but not, as far as is known, accuracy. The important point about these stereotypes, as far as making more accurate judgements is concerned, is to notice any tendencies towards them in yourself, and to question them.

4. *Paralanguage*. Novelists have to convey paralanguage verbally, e.g. ' "You're really amazing", she said irritably.' This channel of NVC includes voice tone and volume, pauses etc.

The main problem in interpreting NVC accurately is its ambiguity. However, *changes* in a person's characteristic NVC are more likely to be significant, e.g. his/her face 'lighting up' when talking about a particular person or topic. For general purposes, Scheflen's (1964) analogy is appropriate: 'a letter of the alphabet does not carry meaning until it is part of a word which is part of a sentence which is part of a discourse and a situation' (p. 324). NVCs are the letters, and sometimes a bit more; interpretations should, therefore, be tentative.

However, other responses can also be made. Consider someone who is swinging her foot (F). You can note F and just bear it in mind or say 'I notice you're swinging your foot'. (In the model of counselling discussed in Chapter 3 this is a challenge.) Or you can say to her: 'You're angry' (strong interpretation) or 'I think F suggests perhaps that you're angry?' (probably more appropriately gentle). Alternatively, and again without interpreting: 'Can you say what F means to you?', or (if you've done appropriate training) 'Try stopping F and putting your foot on the ground. What happens?'.

Conclusions

Type theory is a constructive, anti-oppressive approach to people's remarkable diversity of personality. Its sustained success can be explained by its positive tone, its versatility and the evidence for its validity.

Because it is a general theory, it has wide applications e.g. to career choice, learning styles and communication problems and strategies. The theory suggests ways of preventing clashes, conflicts and misunderstandings. It also explains, at least in part, some clashes, and it suggests strategies for avoiding them and for trying to resolve them.

Generally, we make quite accurate judgements of personality but there is scope for improvement. Some of the obstacles to accuracy were outlined, and strategies for improving accuracy were suggested, primarily treating first impressions as hypotheses and considering alternative interpretations of them.

putting it into practice

1 Check your possible psychological type against the descriptions in Myers' (1998) booklet *Introduction to Type*, which were developed empirically and with particular care.

2 Are there links between your observations of how well you listen (Chapter 3) and your psychological type?

futher reading

Bayne, R. (2004) *Psychological Types at Work*. London: Thomson.

Chapter 1 discusses the strengths and limits of MBTI theory, evidence-based practice and applying the theory ethically and effectively. Chapter 2 introduces the theory in a way that allows self-assessment if desired. The applications chapters are on careers, selection, time, communication, health, coaching and counselling, and leading and managing.

Tieger, P.D. and Barron-Tieger, B. (2001) *Just Your Type*. London: Little, Brown & Co.

Despite the pop psychology flavour of the title and the blurb promising that the secrets of personality type 'can enliven your love life', this is a serious and valuable book. At its heart are guidelines, based on theory, experience and research, for communication with people of each type organised in all the possible pairings and often applicable to non-romantic relationships.

6 | Groupwork theory and practice skills

Introduction

Individuals do not develop and negotiate their personalities, relationships and ways of coping with the world in isolation (see Chapters 1 and 2). From the moment of birth infants are faced with the need to form relationships with their parents who will be the means of providing the warmth, comfort and food essential for survival. Shortly afterwards children's experience commonly includes more than one adult, and often other children. Subsequently they will progress to relationships in the nursery, the school, friends near their home, all of which will provide them with a means of establishing patterns of behaviour, gaining an identity and learning a variety of roles.

So from the beginning we are faced with being members of a group, and as we grow older, the number of groups which are important to us and in which we are important increases. Social workers need to recognise that their clients have a history of belonging to, and being influenced by, a variety of social behaviours. For instance, truanting behaviour in teenagers may be the result of peer group pressure. It may be easier for a child to miss school, and risk the consequences, than go against the other members of the peer group. The social worker must also understand the dynamics (i.e. interactions) in, for example, a family or a children's home, in order to intervene effectively. Further there are behaviours that take place between members of different groups that are the result of social pressure and the most common example is prejudice where a dislike may start without any other rationale than that the other person is a member of a different group. An appreciation of group psychology not only helps with understanding and assessing a client's situation, but also enables social workers to utilise group forces in a therapeutic way.

This chapter aims to summarise the psychological theory of group dynamics (which is referred to again in Chapter 7, when considering relationships within social work settings) and gives a guide to groupwork skills which make use of such theory. The chapter begins by defining the term 'group' and examines examples of the type of study which has contributed to an understanding of group behaviour. Then it looks at the influence groups have upon individual members, followed by the theory concerned with the development and changes in the structure of the group itself (group dynamics). The last part of the chapter looks at why and how social workers might set up a group, and the skills necessary for conducting group sessions.

Definition of the term 'group'

A group can be defined in a number of ways which relate to its function, the nature of its membership (i.e. why people join and whether membership is voluntary) and its goals and eventual purpose. The classic definition by Cartwright and Zander still holds good and describes the group as an aggregate of individuals standing in relations to each other. The kinds of relations exemplified will of course depend on or determine the kind of group, whether it is a family, an audience, a committee, union, or crowd. (Cartwright and Zander, 1968). From this description it becomes clear that there are several kinds of group. It is worth noting this before moving on to consider what is important in the field of group dynamics. Groups can be divided into two categories.

The *primary group* is a group in which members come face to face, regardless of any other characteristics. These groups can be natural groups such as the family, or a group of friends, or they can be formal, like a school class, or a therapeutic group. It is the primary group which is central to this chapter.

Secondary groups are slightly more difficult to identify, but just as important because, even though they do not necessarily come face to face, the potential members have characteristics in common. For instance, they may be single-parent families, the parents of children who go to a particular school, or old people isolated in their homes. (See Twelvetrees (1982) for a discussion of secondary groups in the community.)

The study of group behaviour

The first attempt at an analysis of group behaviour was made at the end of the nineteenth century by Le Bon whose book, *The Crowd* (1920), illustrated his observation that individuals in a large group show behaviour that does not constitute the total of their behaviour as individuals. This means that there appears to be some feature of this large group which cannot be traced to individual members. He considered that some sort of 'collective mind' emerges and that in addition, forces of contagion and suggestibility are at work, and the group acts as if it is hypnotised. In the same year McDougall's book, *The Group Mind*, was published and in *Group Psychology and the Analysis of the Ego* (1922), Freud developed Le Bon's and McDougall's ideas in the context of psychodynamic theory, arguing that the binding force of the group derives from the emotional ties of the members, which are expressions of their libido.

In the USA during the 1930s, social psychologists began to study group dynamics systematically. Kurt Lewin, one of the early researchers, became a very important name in this field. He established the Research Center for Group Dynamics at the Massachusetts Institute of Technology, and the National Training Laboratories in Bethel, Maine. In the UK, psychologists and some psychiatrists became interested in studying groups during the 1940s. The work of Bion, Maine, Jones and others at the Tavistock Institute led to innovations in group psychotherapy, and the study of organisations incorporating psychoanalytic theory.

Other social scientists have made important studies of group behaviour, and it is useful here to distinguish briefly between the particular perspectives from which other disciplines have approached this subject. Sociologists have concentrated on studying natural groups such as the family, work groups, the military, prisons, hospitals, and are concerned with the function and meaning of the social institutions they study. So, for instance, they try to make useful statements about the functions of the family, or the meaning of the family in western capitalist society. Anthropologists have generally employed the technique of participant observation and looked at the way groups live in particular societies. They are more concerned with how people establish their norms and value systems, and the different cultures that emerge. For instance, they might be able to show the significance of the event of childbirth in a society, and the consequent roles and rituals that emerge.

There are four main perspectives employed by psychologists:

1. They are interested in the way groups influence the behaviour, personality, social development, and attitudes of the individuals within them, i.e. the effects of the group on the individual member.
2. They are interested in the characteristics of the groups themselves: how they form, change, develop norms, how they are structured. This kind of study is the one most frequently referred to as the study of *group dynamics*.
3. Deriving from the study of group dynamics and the effect of group pressure on individuals have come studies relating to the effectiveness of particular groups. These studies have been part of applied psychology, and are particularly relevant to education, training and therapy, although they also have applications to less palatable activities such as running prison camps, and torture.
4. There have also been investigations of intergroup cooperation and conflict, with obvious implications for political activity – alliances, warfare, dealing with terrorist activity, hijackers, sieges, and understanding the nature of prejudice.

The individual in the group: social influence

Social influence is the phrase used by psychologists to describe the pressure for *similarity* which is active in all societies. This pressure affects and changes behaviour and attitudes in the direction of prevailing patterns in a particular culture or sub-culture. Although outstanding and unusual people are highly esteemed and a certain admiration is usually afforded to originality, on the whole society values those who share its collective culture and adhere to its rules.

There are three major forms of influence:

Uniformity – which is the similarity which rests on an individual's acceptance of the unspoken assumption that being like others is desirable.

Conformity – which is the similarity that develops when an individual gives in to social pressure to be like others.

Obedience – which is the similarity that rests on compliance with the demands of an authority figure.

There is a great deal of social influence at work within social work teams, which is discussed in Chapter 7. Most people who become social workers' clients are at the mercy of pressures which either cause or emphasise their difficulties. An example is the influence of the peer group on adolescents, which might cause them to deviate from the rules of wider society. Similarly, a father who is out of work, and unable to fulfil the role that his family expect (be like other fathers – be the breadwinner, be dominant, and so on) might see himself as inadequate, his relationships might deteriorate and his emotional health might reach a critical stage.

Psychologists have investigated which particular factors are most important in influencing people towards uniformity, conformity and obedience. The importance of *social norms* in all three areas is clearly demonstrated. Social norms represent the expectations of all members of a society or group. They can be about what is acceptable behaviour in particular circumstances, or about attitudes group members may hold, or about what 'qualifications' members are expected to have achieved. In other words they are rules which represent values which group members consider important, and are thus incorporated into the culture of the society or group.

Social norms may be internally or externally derived. Internal norms are the ones which are particularly relevant to behaviour during social interaction, and are consequently of most concern to psychologists. External norms are those which members bring to the group from their lives outside its influence. Social psychologists have made many studies of normative behaviour; some of these have taken place in a laboratory setting, and others in day-to-day living. For example, Garfinkel's classic (1967) study showed the importance of social norms for people's expectations about each others' behaviour. He hypothesised that there are many unseen rules which govern our behaviour, which we only discover when they are broken, leading to subsequent punishment. He told his students to test these hidden rules in their homes, by acting as 'paying guests' for a period of fifteen minutes. They were to be polite, respectful, and suitably distant towards their families, and only to speak when spoken to. The next day, the students' reports were filled with accounts of their parents' anxiety, astonishment, embarrassment and anger. They had been accused of selfishness and moodiness, and, considering this experiment had only lasted for fifteen minutes and did not constitute openly hostile behaviour, it is an illustration of just how powerful these norms actually are.

Another set of now classical social psychology experiments was carried out by Sherif in the 1930s, and concerned the auto-kinetic effect. This is an optical illusion in which a stationary pinpoint of light viewed in an otherwise dark room appears to be moving. Sherif placed a great many participants in a darkened room and allowed them to make independent assessments about how far the light had moved. He then brought groups of people together and asked them to repeat the task. The group's judgements *converged* on a central estimate of motion, and even when Sherif tested them later he found that group consensus persisted. Thus a social norm was established, and endured despite its lack of authentic foundation.

Studies of the pressure towards uniformity have indicated that the phenomenon of *modelling* is also important. This is copying the behaviour of an influential person, or model, such as a parent, group leader, or pop singer (see Chapter 1). Also, people often judge themselves by seeing how much they agree with other people. This is called social comparison, and contributes towards uniformity. Finally, uniformity is also brought about by the desire to avoid feeling odd or standing out from the crowd. Psychologists have called this objective self-awareness, but it is better described in daily use as self-consciousness.

Conformity may be understood in three ways: first, in terms of *compliance*, when people conform in their behaviour but do not necessarily alter their attitudes. Motives for compliance are often connected with survival, or status and security. An example would be a prisoner who changes his behaviour in order to conform to the rules of the institution (or even to the inmate sub-culture) but inwardly does not alter original hostile feelings. Cohen and Taylor's (1972) study of long-term prisoners showed several examples of this, as did the work of Soloman Asch in a series of experiments in the 1950s. These involved a naïve participant having to say which of three comparison lines was equal in length to a standard line, when all four lines were simultaneously presented. When the individual tackled the task alone there was a high degree of accuracy. However, the naive individuals were then placed in the midst of a group of the experimenter's confederates, who always chose the wrong line deliberately. Asch found that one-third of the time the naïve person agreed with the wrong answer in this situation.

This work demonstrated that individuals are greatly influenced by the pressure towards conformity, even when they probably realise that the group consensus does not provide the correct solution. However, the results of this study have been criticised by other psychologists, who stress that the results should not be generalised: if there was always such pressure to outward compliance then new ideas would never be established, and individual innovations would never get accepted. It has also been found that committed *minorities* in groups can persuade other group members to their point of view, and compliance is thus related to more than majority pressure.

Secondly, *identification* occurs when one person finds it important to be like another. This is referred to as classical identification. Sometimes it is important for someone to meet the *expectations* of another person. This is called reciprocal-role identification, and happens a great deal in marriages or between bosses and secretaries or social workers and clients. Thirdly, a person might be happily influenced by another if he/she finds the behaviour and attitudes of that person consistent with his/her own values. This is called *internalisation*. The influence of a religious leader or charismatic politician is a good example of this.

Interest in obedience increased after the trials of the Nazi war criminals, who claimed that they had committed atrocities as a result of obeying orders, and felt that they should not be held individually responsible for their actions. Stanley Milgram performed a series of what are now famous studies to discover just how far people in general will go when ordered to do something. These are described in his book, *Obedience to Authority* (1974). He set up a laboratory where naïve participants were told that they were assisting in an experiment to assess the effects of punishment on learning. The participant was told that the learner, to whom he was introduced, would be in the next room, wired up to a machine which would administer a shock every time the participant pressed a button. The person was shown a dial which would increase the shock from light to dangerous, and the experimenter told him that he should increase this each time a wrong answer was given. A battery was temporarily attached to a lead, and the individual was given a mild shock just to prove the machine worked. In fact this was the only shock to be administered, as the machine was a fake! Before running his experiments, Milgram sought the views of several psychologists and psychiatrists who said that it would be very unlikely that his participants would continue the experiment after the first couple of shocks.

During the experiment the participants asked the 'learner' certain questions, and when a wrong answer was given, the experimenter told the participant to press the shock button. After a few times the 'learner' started begging the person to stop, and the experimenter told the person to go on, despite the participant's protests. The 'learner' claimed that he had a weak heart, and when the final 'shock' was administered, the screaming stopped, and there was silence. The conditions were varied. Sometimes there was a window so that the participant could see the learner's reactions, at some times the experimenter appeared scruffy and inconsequential, at others well-dressed and authoritative. Milgram thought that these factors might affect the degree of obedience. On average, about 62 per cent of participants obeyed the experimenter until told they might stop, and about 33 per cent proceeded until the learner was silent. Some of the participants expressed great anguish both during the experiments and for some time afterwards, but this was not enough to stop them, and it seems that many people will do as they are told under particular circumstances even though they regret doing it.

Over the past twenty years there has been an important change exacting ethical controls over work in which participants are 'duped' in these ways. However this does not detract from the importance of the work described above.

Group dynamics

Social groups which exert influence over their members are not themselves uniform in nature, but are constantly changing as a result of the influence of individual members and external demands.

Group structure

Once a group has formed, a structural pattern begins to develop, and the role, interpersonal preference, communication, status and power structures emerge, along with patterns of normative behaviour. The developments and changes in these structures are referred to as group processes or group dynamics. The structure of a group may or may not be affected by formal organisations, but, even if it is, informal group structures can be observed. So a team within the probation service has its formal structural relationships dictated by the Assistant Chief Probation Officer, i.e. that the Senior Probation Officer is in charge of the office and makes the major decisions, but informally the Senior Probation Officer may frequently and deliberately enlist the skills of basic grade colleagues in a variety of important tasks.

Groups come together formally or informally in order to perform certain tasks, to be carried out as well as they are able. Groups in which all the members wish to be part, which agree on the tasks to be performed, and recognise the members who are most suitable for each role, are likely to be the most effective. All groups aim at close proximity to this state, but it can rarely be achieved without conflict, and it is this conflict which causes groups to develop and change their structure. A group which is concentrating upon personality or behavioural change in its members might be encouraging everyone to share their fears, anxieties and intimate details of their past lives. If some members do not reveal things in this way, others will feel frustrated and betrayed, and the group will not represent a 'safe' environment for change. The pressure aimed at the 'non-disclosing' members will be manifest in a struggle between the group and individual members about norms, criteria for membership, tasks and roles, and if all eventually agree and feel able to share their intimate feelings, then this is seen as a measure of effectiveness. The process by which the pressure is applied, the alliances which form and the changing patterns of communications, friendship and roles, are the dynamics of the group.

Ralph Linton (1949), one of the first social scientists to consider that a group was an entity, looked at group properties. He felt that these could be divided into structural (e.g. patterns of relationship among members) and dynamic (e.g. expressions of the changes in group relationships) properties; distinct from each other, but closely interwoven. Linton, and also Newcomb (1953), further analysed these properties in terms of status and role structure. The status structures were static, and referred to a collection of rights and duties attributed to the occupant of a particular position in a group. An individual is assigned to a status position and occupies it in relation to other statuses: someone who has been officially designated group leader because of her training in group psychotherapy has a right to occupy this status, because other people are members whose status requires them to recognise the leader's status! The leader also has a duty to use the knowledge and skills which she has, and which have led to her achieving that status. The role structure represents the dynamic aspects of the status position, whereby the occupant of the role puts the rights and duties of her status into effect, and performs the tasks relating to the role of leader/psychotherapist, as in this example.

Linton stresses that status and role are quite inseparable, and that there can be no roles without statuses, and no statuses without roles. Newcomb employed the concept of position rather than status, with the role being seen as the behaviour of people who occupy positions. Every position which is recognised by the members of a group contributes in some way to the purposes of the group, and this contribution represents the group 'function'.

Types of group structure

The affect structure, or interpersonal preference structure, refers to the degree of attraction between group members, and is a powerful determinant of *group cohesiveness*. If attraction between group members is intense, then high value is placed on membership, and the group is said to be cohesive. This may be adversely affected by:

1. an increased number of members, which might mean priority has to be established in power and control of activities, with a greater number of people in subordinate positions.
2. the formation of sub-groups, or cliques, by people who are particularly attracted to each other. This means that an intergroup rivalry will occur within the main group, which will reduce cohesiveness.

The affect structure can be diagramatically represented on a sociogram, a technique invented by Moreno (1934). The sociogram describes who likes whom, who is rejected by the group, who is the most popular, and where the cliques exist.

Most groups are constrained by a communications structure which is imposed upon them. It might be that the area director cannot directly supervise the work of a basic grade social worker, and so she has to do this via the team leader or it might be that a particular residential home has a policy that each worker and residents' views and opinions have to be considered publicly before decisions are taken. Psychologists have studied whether different communications structures hinder the development of group processes or assist in the performance of group tasks. It is apparent that communication structures fulfil different functions more efficiently. The important variable is often the degree of centralisation in a communication network structure.

The wheel is the most centralised pattern, and the circle the least centralised. The wheel facilitates simple decision-making, but is bad for the morale of peripheral group members. For more complex tasks the circle pattern often proves superior. This may be because of more active participation by all members, which itself increases morale, or because in the wheel the centralised person may well be overlooked.

The *power structure* in a group relates to the roles and status positions of its members. There is also an additional component which is related to the influence a member exerts over the others during social interaction. Social power has been defined as 'the potential influence of some influencing agent O, over some person, P. Influence is defined as a change in cognition, attitude, behaviour or emotion of P which can be attributed to O' (French and Raven, 1959). There are different types of powers which can be based on the ability of a group member to reward, coerce, provide expert knowledge, provide information or have other members wishing to be like him/her, or having a legitimate reason for power. Different power is important at different times during the life of a group, and although the sources of power are not independent (one person may have influence through more than one source of power) it is likely that power shifts between members. More recent work has focused in detail upon malevolent use and abuse of power (Kipnis, 2001) which sometimes occurs as part of the informal structure whereby information is 'leaked' or misused to stir conflict (see Kolb and Bartunek, 1992).

As described earlier, the *role structure* represents the dynamic aspects of the status positions. Certain groups have formal roles, such as mother, father, son, daughter, teacher, therapist, and so on, but all have informal role structures in addition. The most important of these are 'leader', 'follower', 'scapegoat', 'lieutenant' (second-in-command and support to the leader). Again, there are various ways in which these informal roles are occupied. For instance the leader may be permanent, short-term, a task leader, an emotional leader. The reason why certain individuals occupy particular roles varies according to the other aspects of structure, group task and personality.

Groupwork

The first part of this chapter has focused attention upon the information available to explain aspects of social behaviour, and reflects upon the importance of a *social existence*. It is important for groupwork leaders to be aware that group members are influenced by the social constraints which have been described, as well as by their own personality and individual histories. Superimposed upon the interaction of the individual group members is the action of group structure and group dynamics: the group itself can be understood independently of the effect its members have upon each other. The leader has to make sense of this aspect of group life in order to be useful to members seeking help and support.

Groupwork in many ways represents a break with traditional social work and its casework relationship between professional worker and client. It has grown in popularity in Britain since the 1960s, partly as a response to criticisms of traditional methods, and partly as a result of emerging as an established force in social work in the USA by 1960. The term 'groupwork' demands a more detailed definition and explanation, especially since within its broad framework there are a variety of models for practice deriving from a diverse body of theory, but at this stage groupwork may be described as 'social work in which one or more social workers is involved in professional practice with a group of probably more than four clients at the same time'. The aims and objectives and the shared characteristics of the members, and the tasks they perform, may vary greatly.

Despite an increase in popularity and a general acceptance of its validity as a method of social work, it is still true to say that groupwork in Britain is a peripheral activity in most fieldwork agencies. Many social work training courses only give it a brief acknowledgement, and it is generally seen as a method of 'prevention' rather than a serious way of dealing with social deprivation. Many agencies expect those of their staff with groupwork skills and commitment to develop groupwork activities as 'spare time extras', which reinforces this belief, even among social workers themselves. Residential and day care institutions tend to value group activities more highly, due to the nature of their work. However, rarely is the work of these institutions seen to have as high a status as fieldwork. We hope this chapter will make a contribution towards persuading the reader of the potential of groupwork *generally* within social work practice.

A social worker should be aware of group influences upon individual clients, and also of changes in the structure of the formal (e.g. therapeutic) and informal (e.g. people in his office) groups with which he is involved. It is important for the social worker to realise that no member either starts or finishes her particular group experience solely as a member of one particular group. Even service users in long-term residential care and prisoners experience diverse effects and reactions to their circumstances, which reflect the influence of other groups to which they have belonged, currently identify with, and aspire to join in the future. Thus all people are influenced by the groups they have contact with, and either choose membership or drop out. In order to function at all, formal groups have to generate norms, even if they are constructed around simple issues such as the length of time group members have to remain together at each meeting. The more effective a group is to become, the more committed its members must be, and this in turn results in a more highly developed and complex set of group norms.

So, in order to sustain its membership, a group must reflect the needs of its members. The social worker setting up a group with highly specific aims and goals might find difficulty in directing the group towards these if the members themselves do not recognise them as their own. Groupwork goals should be flexible, and bear relationships to goals set by members, including the group leader. In order to do this successfully, the social worker has to maintain a grasp of:

● group dynamics;
● the skills needed to set up a group;
● running group meetings so that members are able to explore their own needs and the extent to which that group might meet them.

Groupwork is a generic term. There is no one theoretical or methodological approach which is all-embracing, and the only common feature is that a social worker will be involved in setting up, and probably running, the group: she may or may not be concerned with emotional or environmental change for the group members, and equally may or may not participate in group meetings. The intention of this section is to examine the groupwork skills appropriate to social work, and therefore the focus will be on social work intervention, rather than on group psychotherapy.

A frequently quoted and reasonably adequate definition of groupwork is offered by Konopka (1963). She says that '[s]ocial groupwork is a method of social work which helps individuals to enhance their social functioning through purposeful group experiences, and to cope more effectively with their personal, group, or community problems.' This definition stresses the wide-ranging scope of the method, in that community problems can be dealt with as well as personal and group ones, but an emphasis remains upon the inadequacies of the group members, in that they need to 'cope more effectively' and have particular 'problems' in their lives. Groupwork may also be concerned with non-problem-centred groups such as 'support' and 'consciousness-raising' groups. These provide a chance to explore wider implications of an individual's position in society, and highlight certain features of particular life styles which can be destructive or inhibit growth and change. So for instance, a social workers' support group provides opportunities to explore the position of social workers in a bureaucratic system, the way their clients are treated as a result, and to gain help from, and give help to, their colleagues.

The scope of groupwork

There are many facets of activity which can be included within the term 'groupwork'. These may be divided into several related categories:

1. The method employed by the workers, especially in terms of leadership style.
2. The theoretical basis upon which the group is formed and conducted.
3. The goals of the group according to the worker.
4. The consumers of groupwork, and what they wish to achieve as members.
5. The format of group events – whether they occur regularly, sporadically, are part of institutional life, whether membership fluctuates, and the lifespan of the group, and the nature of group activity (i.e. it is primarily a 'talking' or practical group?)

Based on these components, several models of groupwork have emerged:

● Social groupwork
● Therapeutic groupwork or group therapy
● Community work
● Self-help and support groups.

Within these models there is still opportunity to develop particular approaches. The models are probably distinguished by their focus on a particular section of the potential client population: social groupwork is frequently offered to clients who need to develop their social skills and experiences, such as isolated mothers, or teenagers who are having problems at home or at school; group therapy to people suffering from emotional or psychiatric problems who have identified their needs (or had them identified) as having to change some aspects of their behaviour or emotional reactions; community work usually focuses upon people who identify the root of their problem in terms of environmental deprivation or social injustice, and this model operates in order to help them clarify the issues and work together to effect social change. Consciousness-raising became more popular in the late 1960s and 1970s, with the acknowledgement that social oppression had greatly restricted the political, social and emotional life of certain social groups. The most obvious of these are members of ethnic minorities, women, people with disabilities, children, the working class, pensioners and other sections of society which have learned to recognise the external constraints on their lives and make efforts to understand and change them.

The self-help or support group model is perhaps the widest-ranging in terms of who might benefit. Many self-help groups have emerged, initially under social work leadership. Any group of people with mutual needs or problems may benefit from regular contact with others tackling similar problems. An example of this might be people wishing to set up a playgroup for their own community, a group of ex-alcoholics in Alcoholics Anonymous, or a group of social workers discussing professional concerns (see Chapter 4 for a discussion of peer support).

Embarking upon groupwork

Most social work agencies put little pressure on their staff to undertake any groupwork, and it may well appear that they discourage it by giving work with individuals overriding priority. There are several explanations for this. The basic one is probably that most social workers and social work managers lack training in groupwork, and avoid the possibility of getting out of their depth. There are similarities in the aims and skills of all types of social work, but working with groups of service users can expose the social worker to a potentially threatening situation where she/he will be in the minority, and thus less 'powerful' than in other social work activities.

Additionally for several reasons groups are often best conducted by two social workers, and those groupworkers will be exposing their professional skills to scrutiny which rarely occurs first-hand outside the groupwork role. Although social workers report on their interactions with service users, and seek support from their senior staff, their interpersonal skills are rarely in question. Agencies evaluate social work according to the effectiveness of administration and action in connection with their peoples' lives. Less emphasis is placed upon personal contact and interaction with clients once social workers get beyond their training, and even then, social worker/client contact is generally assessed by way of 'process recordings' or verbal accounts rather than personal observation by supervisors. Similarly, social workers rarely know the details of their colleagues' relationships with their clients, which provides difficulties for assessments of clients' needs in a team with respect to offering groupwork. However, there are several reasons why groupwork might be very acceptable to both clients and staff of statutory and voluntary agencies.

Advantages of groupwork

1. Most people's lives involve situations where they are members of large and small groups. Their experiences result directly from their social position, and therefore it is often useful to confront their problems in a group setting. These are not necessarily emotional problems, but may involve difficulties in a variety of interpersonal settings, e.g. dealing with bureaucracies, people in authority, their own families, etc.
2. All members of the group have certain resources which may well provide help and support for other members.
3. Groups can be made up of people with similar problems and experiences who can provide reassurance, insight and support to each other, in a way professional workers cannot.
4. For people who wish to change some part of their behaviour or personality, a group experience is much more likely to be effective than the traditional one-to-one approach.
5. The social worker is potentially less powerful in the group situation where the other members are always in a majority. Thus his behaviour and decisions are always open to challenge.

6. Certain social worker/service user relationships are traditionally unfruitful. For instance where the prescribed statutory involvement requires control by the social worker over the service user which is usually impossible. Problems may well be exacerbated by the imposed presence of an authority figure, but the service user may be able to confront and deal with them if they can be shared with others in a similar position.

7. There is a likelihood that once groupwork is established in an agency, it will be economical in terms of social work time. Certainly some people will always require some individual contact, either in relation to statutory tasks, or simply because they need to relate to a professional worker, but these contacts could be kept to the minimum.

8. Groupworkers have more chance to gain feedback on their professional ability both from service users and from their co-worker.

Disadvantages of groupwork

1. If members of a group are really going to tackle important issues, they will not have the same guarantee of confidentiality as a one-to-one relationship with a social worker.

2. A great deal of time and effort is involved in setting up and running a group, and often colleagues in an agency may not be particularly supportive.

3. It is necessary to have access to certain physical resources: accommodation, equipment, catering facilities, transport, care facilities for pre-school children.

4. Sometimes, social workers find problems in running groups and may not be able to deal with certain 'explosive' situations which arise, which may be more intense because of the group context.

5. Group membership and selection for membership inevitably results in 'labelling' of individuals as 'depressed mothers', 'school refusers' and so on. There may be a stigma attached to group membership because of this, as selection for membership depends upon individuals having some sort of identifiable 'problem'.

6. Individual members might find that they are not getting as much from the group sessions as they would from a one-to-one session, possibly because one or two other members constantly compete for attention, or they discover that they do not share the same

experiences or difficulties as most of the other members of the group.

7. Particular individuals might experience rejection by the group which reflects their real-life difficulties. The degree to which this may or may not be helpful depends on the commitment of the member and the skill of the groupworkers.

Deciding whether groupwork is appropriate

The decision to start a groupwork project is based upon three separate, but not mutually exclusive factors:

1. The social workers concerned should be committed to groupwork as a form of intervention. This is not to suggest that they are not also committed to other forms of social work, but that they must be convinced of the validity of groupwork itself.
2. There must be some means of identifying and acknowledging the needs of potential group members.
3. Certain basic physical resources must be available.

Most people's experience of social work does not include groupwork, and so prospective group members should be made fully aware of exactly what is being offered.

Setting up the group

Groupwork needs careful preparation. Decisions have to be made which involve apparently endless permutations – the result being that a form of compromise has to be reached by the groupworkers as to:

● who the group members will be;
● the type of group they are going to run (e.g. a 'practical' group or a 'talking' group);
● the length and time of day for each session. Enough time must be available for 'ice-breaking' at each session, despite pressures that the members and workers will probably face concerning their commitments. One-and-a-half to two hours is generally considered suitable. It is also important to take account of the daily routines of potential members, so that a group is not organised mid-afternoon for mothers who have to collect children from school, or an afternoon group for people who are at work;
● the frequency of the sessions and the duration of the life of the group. Many people may not favour a long-term commitment, but

will be happy to meet as frequently as twice a week. For instance, a group for school children during the summer vacation may meet intensively for a relatively short period, enabling them to get to know each other quickly, and so gain the most from the experience. A community group wishing to confront specific problems in an area may wish to meet once a fortnight, as they may be dealing with separate tasks between meetings. It is often a good idea to set a limited number of sessions with the option for the group to review this in the light of experience and achievement at the end of that period.

Aims of the group

The considerations which arise during the planning stages of a group's life must also be taken into account when planning the group's aims. It is important for the groupworkers to be clear about what they plan to achieve and how. These aims may be flexible, and should certainly be reviewed, preferably after each session. This does not mean, for example, that a group for school refusers or bereaved people must constantly focus on the central topic; indeed it may well be that not going to school or the loss is not particularly important for the future lives of the group members. It does mean that a group must set realistic aims which reflect the workers' intentions and abilities, and the members' needs. Being realistic would mean that a group for people attending a day centre for mental health service users would not aim to get the members back into full-time employment in three months. It might, however, aim at enabling the members to take an active part in planning their daily routines, to learn to talk about themselves and their difficulties with each other, and listen to the problems of other members, and it is likely that the group experience would enable them to achieve these aims.

Selecting the group members

Referrals for groupwork may come from a variety of sources which clearly depend upon the agency and type of group. Groups which depend on a system of referral are usually those run by statutory agencies, or those which cater for the needs of a specific section of the population. Some will have methods of self-selection, as in the case of a community-based group, or there may be a method of group selection as in some therapeutic communities. Some groups are non-selective, and these would include 'drop-in' centres, playgroups, and luncheon clubs. They do, however, tend to attract people who identify in some way with the people who regularly attend.

Apart from the referral and selection of members, it is necessary to establish whether a group is to be 'open' or 'closed': whether or not new members should be able to join, and others drop out at any stage. The decision about this rests with the group leaders, and should be clarified before potential members are recruited.

Groupwork in action

The processes and dynamics of each group depend on the leadership and the members, but as we have seen earlier in this chapter, there are also certain developmental sequences which are common to all groups, regardless of the characteristics of members. These relate to group composition and size, group cohesiveness, and conflicts which surround the stated and unstated aims. They reflect the establishment of rules and norms, the degree of commitment and attraction of the members, and the way in which the group processes are handled by the groupworkers. The leader should be aware of the group processes, that is the development of the group itself as distinct from the behaviour of the individuals comprising it. Several groupwork writers have described the stages of group development resulting from changes in the structure which occur in response to the group needs at a particular time. Tuckman (1965) has summarised the sequence of events in group development as *forming, storming, norming* and *performing*, and subsequent writers have suggested a final stage of *mourning*. Groupworkers have a specific part to play at each stage of development, and recognising and understanding the stages will enable them to do this.

Forming. Initially group members will come together knowing very little about each other, and why they are there. They will probably have accepted the leader's explanation that they can share similar problems and experiences with others, but there will be all sorts of doubts and anxieties in their minds about who speaks to whom, when to speak, whether or not to launch into discussion of their problems immediately, or whether they want to disclose anything at all to this bunch of strangers they are now faced with! At this stage the groupworkers play an important part in the interaction. They decide the style of introductions, which set the tone of the first and subsequent meetings. For instance, the leaders might start by telling the group their names, a bit about their work, why they set up the group and what they are hoping it will achieve. They could then ask the members to do something similar.

In practically-oriented groups the workers may assign specific tasks to members, such as setting out chairs, making coffee, buying the provisions or checking the equipment, in order to establish individuals with a role. If the group is one in which members already know each other, as in a hospital or day centre, it is particularly important to stress the aims, functions and boundaries of the group, as distinct from the other activities which members might share. Groups in residential and day care settings frequently do operate successfully, and most people are able to distinguish between their different roles in the group, and in other activities in the same setting.

Storming. Once the members have established who they are and why they are there, it often appears important for some people, or the group as a whole, to rebel against the leaders, or to question the aims and usefulness of the group. It is also frequently true that they will not achieve their aims, or that their problems are insoluble. It is very much a reaction against the initial excitement and optimism on joining a group and meeting others with similar hopes and fears, and then realising that there is more to effective group membership than just sharing these. The group leader has to avoid feeling the same hopelessness, and possibly has to exert more control over individuals than she/he might at some later stage. This is a difficult balance to maintain because too much or too little control could prevent the group from actually becoming a cohesive, effective force in its own right. It is important that the leader questions these attacks and hopeless feelings posed by the members, but does *not* attack the individuals who raise the doubts. It is likely that one or several members will say that they do not feel that sitting in a room for two hours a week will help with their particular difficulties.

Group leaders at all stages, but particularly this one, should respond as much as possible by *opening up* the issues rather than providing a definitive answer. This can be done in a number of ways. For instance, in answer to a personal attack on the leader by a member it might be appropriate to answer by straightforward explanation or denial, but it is likely to be more useful to ask whether other members have seen the leader in the same way, and if the group replies that they have, then the leader might carry on to ask what the group feels she/he could do to make it feel more comfortable. If not the group might focus on why the deviant member feels as he does. Although many people may remain silent during confrontation, if the leader opens up the discussion, other people are frequently able to contribute, and either support or refute the attack. Subsequent discussion may prove fruitful for all involved enabling the group to resolve certain basic conflicts.

Similarly, if a member is 'going off at a tangent', or doing all the talking (often addressing themselves to the leaders rather than to the rest of the group), it is important to try and allow other members to control the discussion if possible. The leader could ask 'What do other people think?', or if this fails, something along the lines of 'It would seem as if Christine has a lot on her mind just now. I wonder if other people have had similar experiences . . .' or 'whether other people can suggest to her how to deal with . . .' If someone senses the group's lack of direction and is allowed to take over, other members may well feel that the group has no place for them, and their suspicions and anxieties will be confirmed. With appropriate 'facilitation' at this early stage, members should be able to deal with over-enthusiastic orators at a later stage of the group's development, preventing the need for too much leadership control over participation.

Norming. During the 'storming' stage, individuals are trying to establish their roles, and work out their values in relation to the rest of the group members. As members become more committed to the group and each other, they establish norms and as a consequence identify with the group and place a degree of emotional investment in its future development. This should not imply harmony – in fact establishing rules and norms by definition implies the existence of transgression. So at this stage there will be people who react against certain accepted norms in one way or another. They may be pushed into the role of 'scapegoat' by the group, which disapproves of their lack of conformity. They may be pressured into compliance, or they may emerge as new leaders, so altering basic group norms.

The group leaders should now be less overtly involved in controlling the direction of the group, and perhaps be providing more in terms of comment and feedback on what they see happening. This is partly in order to allow them to 'check' with the rest of the members as to whether their own perceptions are correct. The leaders will make comments such as 'I feel the group is angry about something, I'm not sure what it is, but perhaps other people sense it also?' or 'I feel the group is concentrating upon things that people are saying rather than the way in which people are feeling, which appears to be quite different because ...' Other members will either agree or challenge the comments, and express the feelings they were unable to talk about. They might not be able to do this if the leader had made statements about the group mood such as 'The group is very angry because Colin arrived late'.

Performing. This is the stage at which the group has managed to develop through its normative processes and changes in role structure, and concentrates upon the major task it has to perform in relation to its individual members, and its own development. Much of this also occurs during the 'norming' stage, and the distinction is often temporal rather than structural.

Mourning. All groups have to end, and some have a natural life, e.g. during the school holidays or during a stay in hospital, and some have deliberately imposed time limits. All endings engender feelings in individuals, and it is important that the group leaders should be aware of this and give opportunities for people to deal with them effectively. There will be a sense of loss and rejection on the part of members when they realise the life of the group is near its end. This may precipitate reactions of withdrawal, or attempts to arrange to see members individually, or informally outside the formal group. The leader should encourage the members to discuss their feelings about ending the group, and allow them to summarise the group development as they see it. They may wish to continue formally, and the leaders may well find it possible and useful to do so, but this will require a return to the planning stage, to decide exactly what the aims and objectives for extending the group might be. Leaders might feel guilty at ending a group, particularly if it was successful, but clearly this is not a reason to prolong its life.

Recording and evaluating groupwork

As with other areas of social work, recording provokes a variety of responses in workers and clients, many of which are unfavourable. Most clients understandably object to details of intimate discussion being written and filed away. Even so, recording is particularly useful for groupworkers assessing a group's development, and in addition, provides the agency with evidence that a valid form of social work is actually taking place! The groupworkers may be helped to assess their own involvement in the group process when they write up, and account for happenings during group sessions, and they should certainly be able to assess individual members' progress. The recording may possibly be made available to the whole group for discussion and referred to as a group 'diary'.

putting it into practice

1 What leadership qualities and style would you apply to working with a group of service users who are suffering from multiple sclerosis? In what ways would groupwork help them?

2 Describe your seminar group or work-related team of colleagues in terms of cohesiveness and power structure. What evidence would you use to construct your theory of this group's structure?

Further reading

Bettelheim, B. (1979) *The Informed Heart: Autonomy in a Mass Age.* New York: Avon.

Bion, W.R. (1961) *Experiences in Groups.* London: Tavistock.

These books both take a broadly psychoanalytic perspective and both emerge from the post-Second World War focus on groups and how they influence human behaviour and mental health for better or worse, and most importantly how the group has a 'life of its own'. Bettelheim's book is an account of his observations of his own and others' experiences in a Nazi concentration camp. Inmates here were experiencing extreme dehumanising conditions and their behaviours and emotions were often unpredictable and frightening.

Bion's work based on studies of therapeutic groups with ex-prisoners of war also shows the power of the unconscious group mind and the ways in which groups defend themselves against processes and experiences that might be difficult or distasteful.

Both of these books bear an important relationship to the further reading in Chapter 7.

part 3 | **The context of social work**

7 | Social work settings and contexts of practice

Introduction

We outlined the main theories and approaches psychology can offer social workers in their everyday practice with service users (Chapters 1 and 2), in developing skills in individual interviewing and group counselling/therapy (Chapters 3 and 6) and self-care (Chapters 4 and 5). Here we examine the way that social workers themselves are subject to the influence of psychological forces in the organisation of their daily working lives. In this chapter we apply psychological knowledge to social work settings and contexts of practice.

Staff relationships and the role of teams

Although social work is a highly individual experience for most practitioners social work agencies arrange their staff in teams. Over the years since this book was first published much has been written about team-working across statutory, voluntary and private sector organisations with the emphasis upon ways that a well functioning team is able to deliver. Research, particularly across business organisations, has been upon leadership, group structures, 'group-think', leader selection, decision-making and dysfunctional teams and almost all studies indicate that a successful team can benefit both the employer and employees and vice versa (Glassop, 2002).

The approach to teams as the context of social work practice here relies most heavily on the theory related to the social psychology of groups and also psychodynamic theories of groups and organisations which feature the impact of unconscious as well as conscious group processes because it seems particularly relevant for social work teams, and because there is already some highlighting of group dynamics in Chapter 6, thus making the optimum use of the theoretical material already introduced.

What is important thus is:

1. Understanding the consequences of the team dynamics to its effectiveness, and the well-being and productivity/effectiveness of the individual worker. It is important for team members to understand the role of the leader and the boundaries of responsibility and for teams and organisations to learn from their own histories and identify positive and negative practices. Anxiety and other emotional experiences which occur when working with others may be best understood via an explication of the unconscious processes (Menzies Lyth, 1992; Obholzer and Zagier Roberts, 1994).

2. The identification of team and organisational cultures, for instance what constitutes 'acceptable behaviour' and pressures to conformity. This has become increasingly important over recent years because of the impact of a series of mistakes in coping with child care and mental health cases where the outcome of inquiries has suggested that some organisations operate a code of silence and 'turn a blind eye' to misdeeds, negligence and incompetent leadership. For example, the case of Victoria Climbié is described in the report of the inquiry headed by Lord Laming (see Chapter 8). The impact of forces towards conformity and obedience was examined in Chapter 6.

3. The processes involved in decision-making groups which are an integral part of the work of social work agencies and once again issues of leadership and culture are implicated in decision-making as well as anxiety and power issues.

The dynamics of the team

There are four major sources of influence affecting the dynamics of the social work team: the first three being mainly conscious processes – group membership, group cohesiveness, and social facilitation – the fourth being the role of unconscious processes.

Group membership. This refers to the nature of the group in terms of how well members relate to one another, share common goals, identify with their colleagues, or whether they merely see themselves as sharing the same office accommodation. Group membership inevitably affects a person's beliefs and activities. As discussed in

Chapter 6, groups exert pressure on their members to conform to particular points of view and ways of doing things, and if individuals do not or cannot share the same values as the other members of the group, they are likely to leave or withdraw emotionally. Membership of the team is important, because it is a source of support to workers who are otherwise quite isolated. If this support is not available it will reduce the quality of the service to consumers: incompatible and unsatisfying work groups have been shown to be a major source of dissatisfaction to workers, and to adversely affect the quality of their work.

Group cohesiveness. This is the term used by social psychologists to refer to the degree to which members are attracted to one another and the group as a whole. A high degree of attraction between members means that value is placed on group membership, and that group is said to be cohesive. Early studies in industrial psychology were concerned with improving the efficiency and the discipline of the workforce. By the 1930s it had become clear to psychologists that the workplace was a social setting, and that relationships at work were very important. Cohesiveness in a work group was found to benefit the workers in so far as their morale increased and they reported a higher level of job satisfaction. However since then the study of organisational psychology has highlighted the centrality of power struggles and conflict (Kolb and Bartunek, 1992; Kipnis, 2001) in all groups and organisations. The way conflicts and power are managed and the quality of leadership in any team influences the quality of work life (QWL) (Glassop, 2002).

Although it may be argued that social work itself can be a satisfying occupation, it is also stressful for much of the time, potentially reducing the QWL, because many service users are likely to be on the brink of a crisis or experiencing chronic suffering. Cohesive work groups enable workers to cope better with stressful situations and improve QWL. It has been found that in a cohesive group, workers confide in one another, and as a result there is less absenteeism and less job turnover. In terms of dealing with the 'bureaucratic' aspects of social work; it has been shown that in cohesive groups the level and degree of communication is enhanced, making for greater efficiency. In Chapters 4, 5 and 6 we discussed the value of peer support, assertiveness skills and understanding group processes for 'survival'.

There are, however, intrinsic forces which prevent groups from becoming cohesive. For example, the more people there are in a team, the more likely it is that only a few will take on responsibility. It is fairly common for teams to include a mix of skills, qualifications and experience which have their impact upon the learning culture. Each person will be an equal team member on one level, but on another have a different degree of responsibility and power. A hierarchy (both official and unofficial) will form. In an hierarchical structure, attraction and friendship patterns are affected, so there may be problems for a group when junior and senior members are friends: junior staff may see the senior person as patronising, senior members are censured by other senior people for 'fraternising', and may distrust overtures of friendship from junior group members, seeing these as flattery or other attempts at manipulation. In addition the impact of gender, ethnicity, age and class on power relations may prevent change and privilege tradition groups militating against development and innovation (Nicolson, 1996).

Promotion of individuals within cohesive teams exacerbates these difficulties particularly if they resemble the existing leadership. If a team increases its membership it is also likely that sub-groups or cliques will form. As we have seen in Chapter 6, groups tend to compete against one another, and membership of one clique increases hostility and suspicion towards another. The existence of cliques is likely to increase secrecy and gossip, reducing the effectiveness of communication. Secrecy may reduce friction, because if knowledge is restricted, those who benefit are less likely to be challenged by those who do not, as they do not know! However, secrecy derogates those from whom the information is kept. Thus large groups are not likely to be cohesive which may reduce QWL and increase stress because of the lack of transparency clearing a way for fantasies to take hold.

Group cohesiveness is increased by any factor which enhances the value of the group to an individual member, such as success in achieving goals. Outside threats tend to increase the group's value to its members. This is particularly noticeable in the face of cutbacks which have been threatened to the budgets of various social work agencies. The staff become much more united in purpose, and attraction and communication levels are higher. The result is also prejudice and hostility towards those outside your own team or clique (see, for example, Dovidio *et al.* (2005) for a discussion of the social psychology of group conflict and prejudice).

Individuals working in the presence of others frequently experience an improved level of work from when they work alone. This is referred to as social facilitation, and has proved to be universal. Social workers who experience themselves as members of a team, may well work more effectively than if they were unaware of the presence of other team members. This effect was first noted in the 1920s, when it was observed that cyclists who were trying to beat the clock on their own improved their performance when competing against others. Subsequent work by psychologists in the laboratory and in field studies has confirmed that when people perform in the presence of others their own performance improves.

The social facilitation effect has been explained in terms of higher psychological arousal experienced in the presence of others, and concern with receiving positive or negative reactions to one's performance. But it may be affected most by the diffusion of responsibility that often takes place in groups. This occurs on occasions when a group effort is to be evaluated, and a contribution expected from everyone. The output is frequently less than would be expected from individual member's contributions. It has been proposed that some members engage in 'social loafing' and do not contribute much as their efforts will not be recognised as emanating from them. This may be reflected in the consequence of team projects, for example a reorganisation of an intake system, which makes the team rather than the individual worker responsible for the assessment done prior to allocation to individual workers: less work may be put into the assessment than if an individual had sole responsibility.

Conformity and obedience

The degree of pressure to which individual social workers are subject is an important consideration when trying to understand staff relationships in fieldwork. The theory relevant to this was discussed in Chapter 6.

Decision-making in groups

Decisions in work organisations frequently evolve from group decision-making. Psychologists have examined the way in which groups actually reach their decisions, that is the group performance and whether this performance demonstrates group effectiveness. That is achieved according to how well the information had been processed and how relevant the decision was to the circumstances. It seems that certain biases are common in decision-making groups and awareness enables these to be avoided. These relate to:

1. The predispositions of the individual members. In an ideal group, each member's attitudes, opinions and beliefs would be discussed openly, and evaluated by the group. Each member would try to understand her colleagues, and the group reach a balanced outcome. Research into decision-making in juries has highlighted the impact that predisposition has upon final voting patterns, and has shown that, in many cases, evidence presented after one has made up one's mind has little impact on final voting, despite persuasive discussion.

2. If a group reaches a minimally acceptable solution to a problem, then group members frequently develop a bias in favour of that solution. So in a committee meeting to consider financial cuts, the solution of reducing the number of administrative staff may be floated, and accepted by the most talkative members. This solution then becomes the one which group members become biased towards and argue to defend, even though they did not necessarily start out by believing this to be the best solution to the problem. There is a general failure among group members to accept criticisms and new ideas, and researchers have found that this is a widespread pattern in groups solving complex problems, like many of those relevant to social work. The actual processes involved in these cases are that several ideas are put forward until a solution meets with some positive response from the most active members. Once there is a minimal agreement, there is a shift in the quality of the discussion with a search towards justification rather than criticism. If new solutions are offered, it is these that are criticised.

Not only are there biases in decision-making groups, but groups also tend to reach polarised decisions. It has been shown that groups will frequently take risky decisions to which individual members themselves are not privately committed. This has been called the 'risky shift' phenomenon. A group of social workers and related professionals might decide to send a child home from residential care to his parents, or decide not to renew a statutory treatment section on a psychiatric patient although privately each individual member of the group might not be prepared to take such a risk alone. Reasons for this might be diffusion of responsibility, or a cultural norm which favours risk, or at least rejects 'over-protectiveness'. Also, group discussions release members from certain inhibitions which they experience when alone. Research into the 'risky shift' effect has also demonstrated that sometimes groups favour decisions which are more conservative than individuals might have made. The main conclusion must be that group decisions tend to be polarised, more extreme than individual members' decisions might be outside the group.

Finally, returning to the effect of cohesiveness in groups, we will focus on the work of Irving Janis. He did research into group decision-making in the late 1960s, when he suggested that cohesive groups are impaired in their effectiveness by 'groupthink'. This occurs when the group's need for consensus overwhelms the members' realistic appraisal of alternative courses of action. Groups of close friends are under a great deal of pressure to agree and do not want to criticise or challenge the ideas of people they like. Janis argues that this may well be disastrous because it limits the number of alternatives, prevents the group from fully examining the action it is taking and avoids seeking expert opinion to support one particular line of argument against another.

There are thus a great many characteristics of social work teams that affect the nature and quality of individual workers' efforts for their service users, and the way policy and practical decisions are made. Despite the apparently individual nature of social work, it is clearly influenced by group dynamics, and an understanding of these processes is useful for professional survival among social workers.

Conscious and unconscious processes in residential and day care organisations

Residential and day care staff work as part of a team, and the same dynamics apply to their inter-relationships as to social workers. However, the residential and day care experience is usually a more intensive one, with the emphasis on group development and the effects of organisational stress.

The nature of the residential task

Residential workers in general do not have the opportunity to remove themselves from residents' lives by doing bureaucratic tasks, as do community-based social workers. Residential work involves constant confrontation with service users' needs and problems. Often the workers see themselves as the cause of some of these problems. Some studies have made significant contributions towards understanding how people deal with these immediately stressful situations. They have been based on the hypothesis proposed by Elliot Jaques concerning social defence systems, which has been developed from the psychoanalytic approach to psychology outlined in Chapter 1. Knowledge of group dynamics and unconscious processes has been developed from studies of hospitals and care homes which have become classic case studies.

Jaques considered that in an organisation the defence against anxiety is one of the primary elements which bind individuals together. In other words, he suggested that within an organisation maladaptive behaviours such as hostility and suspicion will be exhibited, and these are the social counterparts of the symptoms that an individual might exhibit through projection (a concept in psychodynamic theory dealt with in Chapter 1, a defence mechanism which occurs when someone attributes to another person a characteristic which is in fact their own). Thus Jaques sees individuals as externalising impulses which would otherwise give rise to anxiety, and 'pooling' them in the life of the social institutions in which they associate.

One classic study undertaken at a teaching hospital (Menzies, 1970; Menzies Lyth, 1992) illustrates this clearly. This was a study of the way that nurses cope, or fail to cope, with their job, but is relevant to residential workers. Menzies found that the nurses in her study experienced a great deal of anxiety, and set out to understand how they managed to tolerate it. She found that there were two mechanisms for dealing with anxiety: the personal and the institutional.

Individual nurses, by the nature of their jobs, were faced with coping with stress and emotions surrounding the physical care of patients, comforting relatives, comforting patients who were sometimes hostile, and having intimate contact with patients that they might find distressing or even repugnant. In addition, patients and relatives experienced a great many conflicting emotions concerning the nurses: gratitude for the care and attention, envy of their skills and health, and hostility because of their forced dependence. Menzies claims that the nurses project their anxieties into their work situation; because this was unsupportive the nurses were unable to develop coping mechanisms, and so they regressed. This was exacerbated by the 'social defence system' of the organisation, which is the result of each member of the nursing staff's collusion as they operate their own defence mechanisms.

Menzies provides several examples to explain and illustrate this. One of the most important is the way the nurses attempted to minimise their anxiety regarding individual responsibility. Each nurse experienced a powerful internal conflict between the responsibility demanded by her work, and her wishes to avoid this heavy and continuous burden of acting responsibly. This conflict was partially avoided by the processes of splitting, denial and projection, which converted this intra-personal struggle into an inter-personal one. In Menzies' words: 'Each nurse tends to split off aspects of herself from her conscious personality, and to project them into other nurses'. Thus the irresponsible impulses were split off and projected into a nurse's subordinate, who was then treated with the severity which that part of the split-off self deserved. The stern and harsh aspects of herself were split off and projected onto her superiors so that she expected harsh disciplinary treatment from them. It could be observed that nurses frequently claimed that other nurses were careless, irresponsible and in need of continual supervision and discipline.

Defences against anxiety are also defences against reality, when situations become too stressful to bear. However, operating a defence system like the ones that Menzies described requires energy which is deflected from the primary task of caring for the inmates of the institution. Thus residential staff may actually become 'institutionalised' themselves, a phenomenon which is frequently observed. This means that they are less open to new ideas, less responsive to individual needs, and unlikely to create an environment which enables the residents to operate as individuals.

Miller and Gwynne (1972), in their study of residential institutions for people with disabilities and young people with disabling chronic illnesses, used a similar theoretical base. They looked at the primary task of the institution and concluded that society assigns the staff the task of catering for people treated as the 'socially dead' during the interval between this social death and physical death. When people cross the boundary into such an institution, they show that they have failed to occupy or retain any role which, according to the norms of society, confers social status on the individual. However, most staff do not consider the notion of social death as significant, probably because it is too painful. The staff are there because of advances in medicine, prolonging the life of the chronically and terminally ill, because families fail to cope with disabled members and because of cultural changes in society which have deprived it of adequate cultural mechanisms for coping with death (Chapter 2). In contemporary society, death is still a taboo subject despite efforts to change this. Most residential staff in long-stay institutions are committed to caring and probably see themselves as taking on a task with which most people are unable to cope. However this will raise their levels of anxiety and stress. As Zagier Roberts (1994) proposes, the workers had made conscious choices based on idealism although unconsciously they had assigned themselves impossible tasks. Miller and Gwynne demonstrated two models of defence systems which these staff might operate:

The humanitarian defence. Despite social death, there is a pressure of humanitarian values to ensure that the interval between social and physical death is as long as possible: sick people in old people's homes are given medical treatment, even if their life will be reduced in quality afterwards, and staff are not prepared to hear complaints about lack of fulfilment and unhappiness, or their wishes to die.

The liberal defence. Superficially the liberal defence is at odds with the humanitarian defence. The abnormalities of the inmates are denied, and hopes of physical and social rehabilitation are encouraged. However, the truth is soon realised by residents who venture back across the boundary and find they do not easily fit into 'normal' society. Miller and Gwynne found that staff who profess liberal values also tend to 'infantilise' their inmates by claiming they are really normal, but in much the way that babies and children are: they refer to the inmates' activities in a patronising way, realising that they are not normal, but refusing to admit it openly.

Goffman (1968) draws attention to the fact that in long-stay hospitals for people with mental health problems, staff have roles and statuses which are not only recognised internally, but have external meaning: they are not only in the institution to serve the needs of the inmates, and serve society by providing care for its rejects, but are often there to gain professional experience in order to move on to other positions. This is another way individual staff can prevent themselves from becoming overwhelmed by the suffering of the people in their care.

Residential workers, then, appear to face an impossible task, made worse by their own staff and professional networks seeming to deny the reality of the anxiety that this type of work produces. The extent to which people are drawn to this work is related to their need to work through their own unresolved issues (Bion, 1961; Zagier Roberts, 1994). In the next section, the *therapeutic community* model of residential care will be developed.

Residential and day care from the service users' perspective

There are a variety of factors in residential and day care which inhibit or encourage emotional development in consumers for whom they are provided and evidence once again has evolved from a series of classic studies The physical facilities and resources are an obvious influence on the scope of the experience, but probably more significant are the attitudes and behaviour of the staff.

The problematic relationships faced by the staff are experienced at first hand by the consumers. The extremes of regime which are possible greatly affect the quality of life experienced by the consumer. The different models of residential and day care, and their effects, will be discussed in this section. If we are to accept Miller and Gwynne's notion of 'social death', then it can be applied to a greater or lesser extent to most residential and day care institutions. Certainly, people attending day nurseries and luncheon clubs are still very much part of the wider society, but there is also evidence that children in residential care suffer permanent emotional damage from their experiences. It is not 'social death' in the sense of being a state of suspension between being a full member of society and being physically dead, but it does *impair* all these individuals' capacity to live.

This impairment may be in the form of 'institutional neurosis' as described several years ago by Barton (1976) who showed how people who spend a long period in psychiatric hospital adopt certain bizarre characteristics such as strange ways of walking, a lack of interest in their surroundings and a general mood of passivity. All of these features, to a greater or lesser extent, can be seen in consumers for whom attending a day centre is the main focus of their lives, or who live permanently or temporarily in institutions. This is true for children, but studies in residential nurseries have shown a retardation effect in learning and a lack of facility for forming relationships. Reports of older children in residential institutions have demonstrated passivity and dependence in addition to an inability to form lasting relationships. Scott (1992) discussing care for older people in the USA traces the roots of 'anti-institutionalisation' sentiment from the 1950s where he argues that for some user groups it is important to change the nature of the institutional context rather than simply dismantle the institution. Smaller residential care facilities have developed through the private sector in both the USA and the UK which are preferable to many in terms of emotional and physical care than either being in their own homes or in large state funded institutions.

Models of institutions

Miller and Gwynne describe two models of large-scale residential care which correspond with the humanitarian and liberal values previously described. They call these models the 'warehousing model' and the 'horticultural model'. In the warehousing model, the primary task is to prolong physical life, and it translates the model of the hospital into the setting of the residential home. The new resident is defined in terms of physical malfunctioning and is provided with medical and nursing care. The horticultural model caters for an inmate who is perceived as deprived, with unsatisfied drives and unfulfilled capacities. The primary task of the institution is to develop these capacities. The staff provide the residents with opportunities for growth. Miller and Gwynne admit that the horticultural model is an aspiration rather than a reality, being aware of the reality of the work they are doing.

Cardonna (1994) though used the same models as Miller and Gwynne to explore Green Lodge a residential care centre for adolescents with severe behavioural problems. She observed how the warehousing model applied to those who wanted the children to be dependent, well behaved, contained and containable, which they expressed as a need for more discipline and formal organisation. This group of staff saw children as dangerous. Alternatively the horticultural model was employed by those staff wanting to explore and support the emotional needs of the children.

Therapeutic communities

The therapeutic community model has now been bypassed in mental health settings in favour of expediency and cost-effectiveness. However this model of social care and rehabilitation for people with severe mental health difficulties actually made some inroads into tackling the problems of institutionalisation and dependence. Studies of therapeutic communities still have much to offer those concerned with successful caring organisations. The original therapeutic community was the Social Rehabilitation Unit in Surrey, which is now known as the Henderson. It originally catered for ex-prisoners of war who were unable to maintain themselves in society because of social inadequacies. Maxwell Jones, who was the medical super-intendent of the unit, felt that the social relationships of these people needed to be developed, rather than that they should receive medical treatment. He involved staff and residents in the task of providing social feedback on how each of them coped with their work and social routines, which were part of a strict regime.

The therapeutic community model developed by Jones enabled all staff and residents to participate in treatment and policy-making. The 'therapeutic' component was related to rehabilitation to a role in society which was the primary aim, via the 'community', which was the sum of all the people who lived and worked there. The hierarchy was flattened, and responsibility diffused, and thus a sense of community or joint decision-making could arise. In this model everyone is aware of what is happening to everyone else, and is free to comment accordingly. A 'twenty-four hour living learning experience' is what Jones claimed for this approach, and it meant that all interactions between community members had therapeutic potential. The therapeutic community represents a social microcosm – a miniature society – where individuals can practise new roles, and be made aware of their social and interpersonal impact. Residents also had administrative responsibility. All this was done through a rigid network of policy and psychotherapeutic groups, which everyone had to attend, and where they exposed themselves to situations from which they could receive feedback on their behaviour.

This is potentially stressful for staff and residents, but does counter passivity and apathy, and makes people aware of their potential and ability to contribute to their own and other people's treatment, improving QWL. This mechanism, called sociotherapy, involves the treatment and reinforcement of a person's ability to perform roles within the microcosmic society. It is of course difficult to provide any kind of therapy or treatment which does not include an element of coercion, because by definition the person who needs therapy does so in order to be accepted by society, and this only happens if a deviant learns to conform. However, it is the broader use of this model which is of most concern to social workers.

Wider applications of the therapeutic community approach

It has been suggested that there is a difference between the therapeutic community proper, and the therapeutic community approach. The Henderson represents the therapeutic community proper, but other institutions can adopt the important characteristics such as regular group meetings, and a flattening of the hierarchy. It is the opportunity to participate in community decisions, and provide feedback on people's behaviour, that enables most experiences of dependence and passivity to be reversed. Powerful hierarchies can only exist if communication and information are exclusive to particular groups of people. The opening of information provides fairly rapid changes in the nature of institutions.

Martin (1962), describing the therapeutic community approach as it was introduced to a ward of long-stay female psychiatric patients, records how many of the nurses and junior doctors resisted the move to redistribute power. However, the most striking demonstration in his work is the change in the behaviour and emotional responses of the women who had been 'written off' by society. They had developed an interest in their fate and surroundings in the course of a few months.

Adult day centres and residential institutions offered scope for sociotherapy which happened in a variety of settings. The psychiatric profession has neglected to make use of the model, but on the whole social work and specialist educational agencies have been more flexible in finding ways to improve their users' experiences of life. The basis of this model is that it is not the individual in need of treatment so much, but the residential or day care setting itself, which is in need of change. The only change that is to the advantage of the consumers is one which enables them to express their opinions and views and have them acted on where appropriate.

Work with children and young people presents conceptual difficulties as well as practical ones although surprisingly it is in this sector where the idea of therapeutic institutions has been taken up more enthusiastically than with other groups of service users (Obholzer and Zagier Roberts, 1994). Statutory limitations impose restrictions on the degree of democracy which can be introduced in institutions for children, but it is still possible for children to be informed of the circumstances surrounding their lives in care, the fate of the other children they are living with, and to have an equal say in decisions crucial to their own lives. Naturally the aims and objectives of residential and day care settings vary, but most would achieve at least some of their aims by increasing the emphasis on sociotherapy, which entails the use of all the consumer's experiences in assisting emotional growth.

Supervision, emotion and contexts of practice

How do social workers manage their anxiety in these contexts that are potentially hostile, volatile and unsupportive? Fineman (1993) argues that descriptions of organisations, even those which take the unconscious seriously, suggest 'emotional anorexia'. Organisations are treated as if they are rational places where decisions, leaders, goals and functions make sense and follow clear trajectories. The day-to-day reality is that emotions play an important perhaps even a central role in decision-making, strategy and leadership. The role of managers, if they are to improve QWL and to ensure the best provision for the service users, is to support staff and help them manage the emotional content of their daily working lives and, in the case of social work, manage their anxieties.

This is traditionally accomplished through the process of supervision in the work teams. Clulow (1994), using the case of the probation service to explore the dilemmas in managing organisational anxiety for people conflicted about their roles of 'care' and 'control', suggests how that same conflict enters the managerial/supervisory relationship. Being managed and supervised has connotations of not being trusted and setting up a system of surveillance. At the same time staff need help and advice with complex decision-making about service users and their own careers. Clulow argues that a profound distrust of other people exacerbates anxiety about disclosure which can impede learning, progress of practice skills and services to clients. It is therefore incumbent on the manager to enable the social worker to understand and consequently explore the ways in which their work and discussion of their emotions and their impact upon relationships are direct parallels to their work with service users. In a supervisory role the manager should be able to access the 'big picture' as well so that the social worker can relate interpersonal practices, emotions and organisational dynamics (Holloway, 1995). For this reason supervision needs to be explicitly about learning and the manager/ supervisor also needs to benefit from a similar experience but, in addition, to recognise the value of being a supervisor for her/his own development.

The relationships between team members with their peers, juniors and managers are in constant need of attention in all organisations but never so overtly than in one which works to support and change people. The workers need to acknowledge the same ethos in order to build and maintain the effectiveness of their teams. This requires both honesty and a degree of bravery because for all of us this demands challenging our own resistance and facing the anxieties within ourselves that are brought out in the context of a social care organisation.

---

putting it into practice

1 *Observation of group discussion.* Make notes about either a seminar group or a team meeting (although it is ethical to let members of the group aware you are doing this) and identify the ways in which decisions are made. Who makes a proposal for a solution to a problem? At what stage in the meeting is a proposal made? Are there counter proposals? What factors lead to a proposal being adopted? Are they about the force with which the proposal is made, who makes it, who supports it and so on?

2 *How has being a member of this seminar group or team influenced you?* Have any group norms affected the way you think about things or your practice? Have you experienced any changes (positive or negative) in your self-image as a consequence of group membership? How do you know that it is the group that has influenced these things?

Further reading

Fineman, S. (1993) *Emotion in Organisations.* London: Sage.

Menzies, I.E.P. (1970) *The Functioning of Social Systems as a Defence against Anxiety.* London: Tavistock Institute of Human Relations.

Menzies Lyth, I.E.P. (1992) *Containing Anxiety in Institutions, Selected essays, Volume 1.* London: Free Associations Press.

Fineman's edited collection highlights the fact that organisations are not rational although their overt aim is to ensure that the employees work effectively to ensure the development of the 'product'. However, when people work together either cooperatively or in competition it is impossible to achieve the outcome of a successful product without distress, greed, vanity, anxiety, fear and conflicts of various kinds being part of the process. Menzies' classic work which investigated the reasons that trainee nurses left their jobs either during or shortly after their training identified various unconscious defences used by the individual and the organisation which were the result of a highly stressful occupational role.

8 | Social policy, social work and psychology

Introduction

As we have shown in Chapter 7, research in psychology (as in any other discipline) is shaped by political decisions and by social contexts, both in terms of 'what we need to know' and what is recognised as reliable 'evidence' at any particular time. Practitioners need to develop their own critical and reflective skills in order to evaluate and apply research findings in specific settings (Gomm and Davies, 2000).

Here we examine the inter-relationships between social policy, social work practice and research in psychology. We look firstly at the relationship between social policy and notions of children's best interests, using this as an illustration of the ways in which these have fluctuated radically over the last two generations. After this, we highlight some recent changes in the relationship between agencies, service users and professionals which are shaping the ways in which psychological research related to social care is planned and interpreted. This lays a basis for a further discussion in Chapter 9, reflecting on new initiatives to promote 'knowledge-based' or 'evidence-based' practice in social work.

What's best for children? Changing views of 'mother' care and 'other' care

Modern child care policy had its origins in the late 1940s with the creation of the Children's Departments. Since then, ideas of 'what is best' for children have fluctuated, sometimes seeming to come full circle. The relationship between expert psychological advice, policy and practice has sometimes been deeply problematic. A series of tragic incidents such as child deaths, for example when young children have experienced severe neglect and abuse in the family home, has prompted major re-examinations of social work roles and processes. Maria Colwell died in 1973, during a period in which policy prioritised the view that children should be with a natural parent (or a close relative) if at all possible; nearly 30 years later, Victoria Climbié died in 2000 as a result of neglect and abuse, again while in family care (with an aunt). In both cases, formal inquiries followed and new directions in practice and service organisation were debated (for a detailed discussion, see, for example, Parton, 2004). The case of Victoria Climbié has led to major changes, through an increased emphasis on inter-professional collaboration and preventive work outlined in the government's Green Paper *Every Child Matters* in 2003, and the subsequent Children Act (DfES, 2004). We return to this briefly in Chapter 9 (p. 172). However, both events, as well as a series of other tragedies and inquiries in the intervening years (Parton, op. cit) occurred while practice was heavily influenced by a particular psychological model of family relationships, as well as by problems arising from professional and agency boundaries and resources. In this first section of the chapter, we illustrate some of the ways in which notions of attachment and appropriate care have proved both changeable and susceptible to political and economic imperatives.

Is 'family' best?

Do women have a 'maternal instinct' which propels them towards motherhood and makes them protect their offspring even at the risk of their own lives? Are 'natural' parents or relatives generally the best carers for children from a psychological point of view? Such a view has been economically and politically expedient at particular times (as we shall see later, p. 152); however, it has no scientific basis (see Chapter 2).

To take one example, Badinter (1980) clearly demonstrated, through an historical analysis of motherhood in France, that mothering takes socially and culturally specific forms: it is not an unvarying, instinctual form of behaviour. Tizard (1975) and other writers have drawn attention to Bowlby's work, which has probably been the most influential research on child welfare in the mid- to late-20th century. This example also demonstrates how specific research findings tend to be taken up and amplified when they suit the political and economic climate; in turn, a changed social context allows room for new or previously marginalised social and intellectual interventions. Certain aspects of Bowlby's work have been mentioned in Chapter 6 (attachment); for social workers and their clients the consequences have been a fundamental influence on attitudes, behaviour and provision regarding child care.

Bowlby (a psychoanalytically-oriented psychiatrist) drew on research in the post-Second World War period to argue that the mental health of infants and young children was dependent upon the experience of a warm, intimate and continuous relationship with their mother, or a permanent mother substitute. In its absence, 'maternal deprivation' resulted in delinquent, psychopathic or other personality disorders. Bowlby's evidence was gained from studies of children in residential institutions and hospitals, and from case studies of children who experienced separation due to wartime evacuation. Some of his work was retrospective, based on work with disturbed children for whom he traced a link with inadequate maternal bonding. His findings were supported by other studies, which looked at emotional deprivation in children in French orphanages.

Despite the sources of his evidence, derived from institutions which arguably made deeply inadequate provision for the emotional development of children in their care, the conclusion drawn by Bowlby and others from his work was that the separation of a young child from its mother was in itself a bad thing. Tizard contends that such was the impact of Bowlby's work that this notion almost assumed the status of a *law* in psychology. As such it was used in arguments for closing day nurseries, despite the fact that no studies had been published which demonstrated ill effects arising from day nursery care.

It is now acknowledged that Bowlby's work was used after the Second World War to encourage women who had taken essential jobs in factories as part of the war effort to relinquish them to returning men. Women were persuaded of the permanent damage that their children would suffer if they did not offer them full-time care. The American film *Rosie the Riveter* illustrated this dramatically, by contrasting the pre-war propaganda shown to American mothers about the *benefits* of day care for their children, with subsequent campaigns telling them of their selfishness, cruelty and maladaptive sexuality if they had not returned to their 'natural' role as full-time mother. An academic overview of this theme can be found in Alcock *et al.* (2000).

For children and families in need of social work support, the impact of Bowlby's work was to contribute to the prioritising of preventive measures rather than the removal of children from troubled family homes into residential or foster care. Such an emphasis had been discussed as early as 1946 by the Women's Group on Public Welfare (a subcommittee of the Curtis Committee) which had looked at 'the meglected child and his family'. They argued that the removal of a child from his or her family was an easy answer to an unsatisfactory home, but not psychologically sound in terms of the child's emotional life. There were also concerns with the substantial costs incurred by providing both residential and foster care. The Women's Group proposed the radical suggestion that an 'intensive family casework service' might provide ways of helping families stay together. This is well supported by Bowlby's thesis that continuous care, preferably from the child's mother, is best for his or her future mental health. Thus child care officers were trained in 'preventive' work, and in 1952 legislation was passed to enable them to intervene in a family if they were not going to remove a child: the 1952 Children and Young Persons (Amendment) Act gave local authorities the right to enter the homes of children who were likely to be at risk of going into care, in order to undertake casework. This was justified by the psychological concept that separation from the natural parent increases a child's deprivation.

Those who advocated 'preventive casework' were also of the opinion that if financial pressures on families were reduced, then casework might enable families to modify their existing capacities for relationships and provide a suitable environment for child care. Thus, in the 1963 Children Act, local authorities were empowered to provide material and monetary aid for families, which was important since the National Assistance Board was frequently too inflexible to provide additional help for deprived families. The implementation of this Act meant that more children were supervised at home than were received into care, and it increased the complexity and workload of the Children's Departments.

Experience soon demonstrated that children suffering from neglect often had parents with similar backgrounds. Local authorities were intervening in families where adequate emotional and physical care could not be provided; this raised the possibility that social workers could find themselves reinforcing a family's entrenched difficulties, unable to prevent their effects on subsequent generations. From a psychological perspective, it is clear in retrospect that the training and expertise of child care officers did not equip them fully to weigh the dangers of *separation* for children from their parents against the *physical, material or emotional neglect* they might be suffering, and to be equipped with a variety of possible solutions. Nevertheless, statistics show that the emphasis during the 1960s and 1970s remained on prevention, reflecting the dominant beliefs of the era rather than a more dispassionate assessment.

Broader models of care and attachment

Shortly after the publication of Bowlby's findings and their ensuing impact, other studies like those of Schaffer and Emmerson (Chapter 2) and later Scarr and Dunn showed that children were capable of forming multiple attachments by the age of 6 months. We also know that a child can benefit from forming several attachments, and their social skills in this actually improve with practice. During the 1970s psychologists started to focus on the *benefits* of multiple attachments; by then, with the emergence of the 'second wave' women's movement and other social movements, there was a more positive climate for research which questioned one-dimensional views of attachment as well as gender roles themselves. In 1972, Michael Rutter's influential *Maternal Deprivation Reassessed* was published, since updated in new editions in 1981 and 1991. In other examples, Eckerman and Whatley (1977) showed the importance of the peer group for emotional and intellectual development among children. They demonstrated that 10 to 12 month old children will play with each other, and although no *attachment* appears to form, they are not indifferent to their peers. Mueller and Brenner (1977) emphasised the importance of practice in social relationships in 1 to 2 year olds, and Hartup (1970) showed that 3 year olds and above have 'best friends'. We return to these themes again, in connection with current debates about employment and child care.

Other research in the same period has demonstrated that in some circumstances it may actually be damaging for some children to rely solely or mainly on a close and continuous relationship with one person. This can lead to the child suffering in some ways from the problems that this person experiences: for example, one study found that the accident rate for children with depressed mothers was four times higher than that of children whose mothers were not depressed

(Richman, 1976). Mothers in this study reported loss of interest in their children when they were depressed and anxious. Richman also found a link between the mental and emotional state of the mother and the child's development. Mothers who were depressed were most likely to have children with behaviour problems. She asserts that even if they do not exhibit problems, they are less likely to be stimulated by a depressed mother.

Permanent substitute care: adoption, fostering or residential care?

Turning to a different example within the field of care for children, assessments of the relationships between natural parents and children were challenged again after the Seebohm Committee's recommendations in 1971 resulted in Social Services Departments (SSDs) being formed from existing welfare services (Alcock et al., 2000: 235). Shortly afterwards (in 1973) the death of Maria Colwell, who had been returned to her mother from foster parents by social workers, resulted in the Houghton Committee Inquiry. The report expressed concern for children who were suffering because bonds with their natural parents were being preserved at all costs.

The 1975 Children Act emphasised the need to protect the child's interests above all others, making explicit the possibility that these may conflict with the needs and desires of birth parents. BASW refers to this as the 'adversary model' and understandably expressed the fear that changes in legislation to this effect could well ignore the subtleties in attachments between parents and children. Parents might, for instance, be discouraged from requesting voluntary receptions into care because they feared that admitting the need for any support or respite might expose them to the possible permanent loss of their children. The Children Act, of course, gave increased powers to social workers to make decisions about what form of care would be in a child's 'best interests'.

In this connection, it is also worth looking briefly at how the relative benefits and disadvantages of different forms of substitute care – foster care, adoption and residential care – have been assessed at different periods. In the post-war climate, residential care came to be associated with significant problems: the Curtis Committee's 1948 report focused upon the poor quality of residential child care institutions. There were various psychological research reports which suggested that institutional care from infancy was likely to result in retardation of cognitive skills and intellectual development, as well as impaired emotional growth (e.g. Spitz, 1945). Foster care had the advantage of much lower costs as well as a family setting, but here too an inquiry into a child's death became one of the milestones: the Monckton Inquiry of 1945 into the death of Dennis O'Neill, after mistreatment in a foster home, focused on problems with the selection and administration of foster carers.

However, the Curtis Committee presented evidence that children in foster homes seemed to be more integrated into society than children in orphanages who experienced the effects of segregation. Curtis reported that children in foster homes were less starved of affection and more independent than those in residential care. These findings were given extra significance by evidence from the work of John Bowlby, as described above. Overall, it was a generally-held belief that substitute care for children was provided for love rather than money, and that high rates of pay for foster parents might become associated with child exploitation, so payments to foster parents were kept low. This cannot be divorced from a context in which the notion of a 'family wage' – earned by a male breadwinner – was still the norm, and in which few women could access well-paid employment or careers. In the early 1950s there was a great deal of pressure on children's departments to save money on the number of children they had in care in England and Wales, which had increased by 10 000 between 1949 and 1953. Therefore an economical solution had to be provided. This tied in with current psychological evidence that institutional care was damaging, as well as with prevailing norms concerning care as 'women's work'.

Even so, it is notable that the rationale for the development of family-based foster care (and also adoption) was based mainly on the research evidence related to the negative effects of residential institutions, and not so much on any identified benefits of family-based care. It was also clear that improving residential care would cost much more than increasing the supply of foster homes; in this context, no evidence on how institutional care might be improved, or even be of ultimate benefit to children, was presented. This resulted in the long-term decline of the children's home: residential staff received less money and training than colleagues in other settings, and recruitment in this area declined in quantity and quality. By 1963, the Williams Committee found that only 15 per cent of staff in local authority children's homes were qualified. Fieldworkers had much higher status, and morale among residential staff dropped. It has remained so since, with very few exceptions. Later recommendations to improve conditions for residential and day care staff, were eventually made, by the Barclay Committee Report in 1982 (discussed again below, p. 163).

However, it is within the realms of most social scientists' imaginations to see that a high-quality residential experience might provide opportunities that family life cannot, in terms of adaptability to a variety of social relationships, understanding the implications of living with other people, reducing desire to compete and seek attention, and other socially-oriented characteristics. (This argument was proposed by Lee and Pithers in *Radical Social Work and Practice*, 1980.) The introduction of these points in this context is to demonstrate that social policy is not value-free in the way it selects psychological evidence to support decisions; and that the major impetus behind the expansion of fostering is more likely to have been economic than a result of psychological research.

Since the Children Act of 1975, a series of reports and Acts of Parliament have led to children's needs generally being assessed on an individual basis, with safety and child protection issues overriding 'psychological' ones. Social services departments have evolved specialist services concerning children and child protection. This is as a result of the inadequacies highlighted by inquiries into cases of child abuse, and the frustration many social workers have felt in not being able to 'specialise'. New specialist services have included social workers and social work teams with responsibility for child sexual abuse, non-accidental injury, and specialist fostering and adoption workers.

A useful, overall review of psychological research perspectives on substitute care of all kinds for children has been provided by Michael Rutter (2000). He notes the general under-resourcing of all forms of substitute care, in a context in which high-quality child care of all types has generally been a low policy priority:

The basic question here perhaps is why does society value childcare so little and what should be done to change this? ... the facts are that financial rewards for providing childcare of all kinds are set at a low level, many of the criteria for acceptance as foster parents are undemanding and the arrangements in society as a whole with respect to careers of parents and tax arrangements give little or no priority to childcare.
Rutter, 2000: 694

Rutter notes new evidence that genetic factors may play a part in patterns of family well-being and neglect, although he emphasises the importance of the complex interplay between these factors and the social environment. He also finds evidence of 'resilience and recovery' among children who have experienced neglect in the family home, across care settings which range from group residential care to fostering and adoption. His overall conclusion is that there has been a lack of systematic research in key areas; examples include both the lack of a thorough assessment of the advantages and disadvantages of residential care (for instance, for troubled adolescents who may find fostering or adoption very difficult), and gaps in research concerning what is meant by 'matching' children with adoptive parents (for example, in terms of ethnicity and culture, where until recently a somewhat simplistic concern for political correctness has resulted in limiting the availability of adoptive parents for minority ethnic children – and therefore prolonging their stays in residential care).

The most recent concerns which have been raised about child protection are about the dangers of a lack of coherence and communication between the different services and professionals working with children. In response, children's services have been reshaped to include more joint working between education, social services and health care, partly through the creation of integrated Children's Trusts as well as a range of other measures (DfES, 2004), and we touch on this again in Chapter 9.

Child care, employment and welfare policies

Lastly, we return to the theme of nursery care for children, and to the continuing debate concerning childcare provision and its advantages and disadvantages for children, families and communities. This, then revolves around the perceived needs and experiences of 'ordinary' families, not only on those seen as being 'at risk' in specific ways. Rather presciently, psychologists Sandra Scarr and Judy Dunn wrote that:

> Battles over how women can work outside the home without sacrificing their children's welfare will be fought in decades to come. There will be battles about the low status and poor pay of typical women's occupations, many of which involve work with children. There will be battles over the legitimacy of childcare, its standards, its availability and who shall pay.
> Scarr and Dunn, 1987: 45

Belsky (2001) and others have stressed the need for psychologists working in the area of day care for children to carry out in-depth research on the impact on parents, families and the social structure. To date, there have been a range of developments: as in other areas, there are differing examples of 'evidence' for social workers to evaluate. Whereas in 1981 only 24 per cent of mothers in the UK returned to paid work within a year of childbirth, the percentage had risen to 67 per cent by 2001; day nurseries have become the most common form of care for children under three (Madeleine Bunting: 'Fear on nursery care forces rethink', *Guardian*, 8.7.2004).

In the 1970s, research was done to see whether there was evidence that children at day nurseries do suffer from 'maternal deprivation'. Willis and Riciutti (1974) studied infants aged 4 to 15 months of age, observing their arrivals at day nursery over a period of 6 months. Most babies greeted the nursery nurses with pleasure, or without distress, and at the end of the day greeted their parents happily. Although Ricutti concluded that children preferred their mother, they had also developed an attachment to the nursery worker. These studies, if taken seriously, go some way towards refining understandings of attachment and well-being.

The debate has continued, with a useful overview (*Mother Care/Other Care*) by Scarr and Dunn in 1987, for example, emphasising the difference between high-quality day care and institutionalisation. Alcock *et al.* (2000) illustrate the ways in which current social policy is based on the assumption that most mothers are now also in paid work (often part-time), rather than being based on the assumption of a male breadwinner; however, mothers are also assumed to remain the central carers in the family, in a context of an unequal division of emotional and household labour. Zoritch *et al.* (1998) report good outcomes for children attending day care, in terms of school attainment, development and progress in later life. More recent findings from two major longitudinal studies do suggest some concerns, however: for example, group care appears to be associated with good outcomes when attended by children over two, but not for those who attend aged under two, even where the hours of attendance are low and the quality of care is high (Sylva *et al.*, 2003). If these findings are confirmed in further studies, it will be interesting to see whether or not they have any impact on UK government social and economic policies, which continue to encourage both parents to work outside the home relatively soon after a child's birth.

Moving beyond policies on child care and employment, research drawing on Bowlby's work has now moved away from the simplistic interpretations noted above, and has come to inform wider aspects of social work in terms of family support. Turney and Tanner (2001), for example, have proposed an intervention model for family support in cases of child neglect, drawing on attachment theory to help social workers to develop a model which acknowledges a range of parenting styles.

The policy and practice developments outlined briefly above show how 'evidence' from psychology may be mobilised in contrasting ways, depending on the arguments or policy pressures which gain prominence at a particular time. We now move on to highlight some general changes in policy and practice directions which are influencing the context for *producing* psychological research, and for adopting research findings in day-to-day social work practice, through a consideration of the relationship between agencies, social workers and those who use their services.

Changes in the relationship between agencies, service users and social workers

The period since the Second World War has seen the growth of the profession of social work, characterised by different phases of development and changing emphases. Each new phase has brought a degree of reorientation in response to social policy and economic changes, but each has also involved changes in the attitudes of social workers towards the use and relevance of psychological theory.

From the 1950s to the 1970s: professional development and the tension between individual casework and community work

Social work in the post-war period involved professional development and training with an explicit emphasis on psychodynamic approaches and individual casework, informed by psychological theory. However, this was followed by a 'sociological' reaction and the growth of community work in the late 1960s and early 1970s, accompanied by a flirtation with the 'systems approach'; now, social workers were required to make some sense of social institutions and of social relations at a structural level (e.g. regarding gender and social class) as well as of the individual behaviour of their clients. These approaches could be seen as complementary, in fact, but tended to be seen as competing alternative paradigms instead.

Later, social work agencies responded to increasing limitations in their resources with an emphasis on task-centred work and crisis intervention. This emphasis on expediency frequently meant that a consideration of the social causes of individual or family problems received less time and attention than they deserved, with a corresponding marginalisation of psychological knowledge. This phase, occurring at the end of the 1970s, coincided with the time when many voluntary agencies, particularly those concerned with community work and prevention, offered a space for innovative practice. Accordingly, these organisations were sometimes classed as agents of 'radical' social work and certain local authorities began to withdraw resources. At the same time, radical networks themselves were sometimes hostile towards psychological expertise, feeling that it represented an emphasis on individual problems and deficiencies at the expense of addressing poverty and inequality at a social level. For example, in 1976 the Association of Community Workers stated that 'conventional individual and social psychology offers little help to community workers who work with a range of normal individuals ... in a variety of roles'. They criticised social psychology not only for its content (e.g. effects of the mass media, effects of collective action) but also because little work had been done in 'natural' rather than experimental settings. Arguably there were some important missed opportunities for collaboration here, in a context in which psychology did not become usefully or critically incorporated into social and community work education, but instead came to be seen as an outmoded and reactionary discipline.

Later writers (e.g. Twelvetrees, 1982) progressed beyond this impasse, encouraging the integration of literature on group behaviour and groupwork into community work theory, and stressing that understanding group processes can contribute to community workers' awareness and skills concerning appropriate interventions. He also emphasised the point made by Goetschius, that it is important for a worker to help a community group to evaluate its own work and to decide how to progress without repeating mistakes. Again, Twelvetrees emphasised that action and social change can be combined with understanding the emotional side of people's lives: individual members of community groups experience a variety of emotional and psychological reactions, as well as experiencing structural problems such as discrimination or poverty. It is important for community-based workers to make sense of these as part of an overall support and facilitating role.

The 1980s and 1990s: managerialism and 'quasi-markets'

It has been argued that a 'mixed economy of care' has been in place in one form or another since the establishment of the welfare state (Cochrane and Clarke, 1993). Families, state-funded public services and private or voluntary organisations have all contributed to providing specific services, such as care for children or for older people; however, the proportion provided by each one, and the ways in which they have been expected to collaborate, compete or coexist, have varied dramatically. Fiona Williams (1993) has argued that one way to understand changes at this level is by focusing on the fluctuating relationships between 'family', 'work' and 'state'.

The 1980s brought a major shift in these relationships, when the Conservative Government set out to decrease the role of the state in funding health and welfare services; policy initatives were now framed in terms of encouraging individuals and families to 'take responsibility' as far as possible, and also to exercise choice. Competition between alternative sources of provision was seen as a lever for improving quality; the 'professional self-regulation' which had tended to characterise arenas such as medicine and social work was challenged (Davies, 2000). This represented a break with the post war political consensus which underpinned the creation and maintenance of the welfare state. Now, SSDs took on new roles in commissioning, purchasing and managing 'care': for example, rather than running their own residential homes for older people, new funding arrangements caused them to close these and to purchase services from private care homes instead. Within a structure of contracts between purchaser organisations and provider organisations, individual 'clients' now became 'consumers', and this context was explicitly compared with a commercial marketplace. Researchers commonly termed these public service developments a 'quasi-market', since the forms and levels of choices could not be seen as truly mirroring those which people make when buying other goods and services (Ferlie et al., 1996). For example, most people would agree that an admission to hospital or to residential care entails meeting a fairly complex 'need' rather than making the kind of consumer 'choice' involved in buying a washing-machine or paying a decorator.

In 1982 a working party set up by the National Institute of Social Work (the Barclay Committee) reviewed the role and tasks of social workers in SSDs and related voluntary agencies. Its report stressed the importance of mobilising community resources and informal care, reinforcing a shift for SSDs from a 'provider' role to an 'enabling', purchasing and managing one. In addition to an emphasis on caring for people in the community, it proposed the idea that community social work could be put into practice by using residential and day care institutions as community resource centres.

To date there has been little formal research into the psychological effects of these changes on service users and their relatives; most research has addressed organisational effects or changes in service quality. The Barclay proposals did also contribute to breaking down the rigid distinction between field and residential workers, because residential and day care establishments became the focus of much community-oriented social work. Over this period, many local authorities cut back completely on community work posts (as distinct from social work posts): the emphasis shifted to managing 'packages of care' which could be delivered by a range of staff – a move which many social workers found unwelcome and problematic. At the same time, however, concerns with patterns of inequality and discrimination led to the promotion of 'anti-oppressive practice' in social work – acknowledging differences in power relations, on the basis of class, gender, ethnicity, age and disability. While these initiatives themselves came close to becoming a new kind of 'politically correct' orthodoxy at times, they did stimulate continued attention to social as distinct from individual contexts (Wilson and Beresford, 2000).

From the 1990s: 'modernisation'?

The most recent phase has been characterised by the Labour Government's initiatives to 'modernise' social services since 1997, as part of the Labour Party's 'third way' in politics. Distinct purchaser and provider roles have remained, but the emphasis on competition has been replaced by an emphasis on target-setting, accountability and performance management (see, for example, Tilbury, 2004). There has also been a new emphasis on collaboration and partnership, both at the inter-professional level and at the inter-agency level (Hudson, 2002). This is seen both as promoting cost-effectiveness and also as helping to manage risk: for example, by improving communications across agencies with respect to child protection and to mental health. In this context, new 'area-based initiatives' have become a focus for social work collaboration with healthcare and voluntary sector organisations. The 'Sure Start' programme, for example, has funded new roles in family support and in outreach work with fathers, designed to offer 'one stop shop' and outreach services for families with young children in areas of deprivation, and to take the pressure off professionals – including social workers – by undertaking some of the preventive work formerly offered by SSDs. While no doubt driven by policy concerns with containing both costs and risks, these initiatives do in fact offer considerable scope for practitioners to overcome long-entrenched polarisations between psychological, medical and sociological models and theories. For instance, there are genuine opportunities for discussion between social workers, health visitors and family support workers about psychological models of child development and parenting styles, and their implications for practice.

Lastly, the two most recent phases have been accompanied by increasingly prominent challenges and interventions from users of social and health care services. The consumerist emphasis on individual choice and purchaser-provider contract of the 1980s has been met with a reassertion of notions of citizenship and collective rights, from academic, professional and user vantage points – although the 'consumer' agenda has also been seen as a welcome opportunity to challenge a long-established paternalism in public services (Barnes, 1999, 2002; Beresford and Croft, 2001). The term 'service user' has come to be accepted by many in social work as a substitute for client (or 'customer' or 'consumer'), and as a workable compromise:

> The term 'service user' is problematic, because it conceives of people primarily in terms of their use of services, which may well not be how they would define themselves. However, there is no other umbrella term that can helpfully be used to describe all these overlapping groups.
> Beresford and Croft, 2001: 312

Networks of people with disabilities, in particular, have taken a leading role in redefining the relationship between users and providers of services as one which should (as far as possible) be characterised by mutual respect, partnership and dialogue. In terms of research in psychology as well as in other disciplines, this has begun to have an impact on what is defined as an interesting or important area of inquiry, as well as on research designs and processes: people with disabilities, for example, have collaborated with academic researchers on studies examining new initiatives in independent living. This is a substantial departure from earlier focuses on institutional care, and it has challenged the previous stigmatisation of people with physical and intellectual impairments (Gibbs, 1999; Barnes, 2002).

Conclusions

In this chapter, we have noted a number of examples in which the social and economic context has prioritised some aspects of psychological research and marginalised others. Since the 1970s, policy and funding developments have increasingly required that social workers extend their practice beyond concern for interpersonal relationships. Psychological theory incorporated into social work training and practice needs to be developed and understood accordingly, making links with political and sociological perspectives at the same time. This means that social workers will need to be familiar with *more* psychological material, with an increased critical facility to select and integrate relevant knowledge and skills. In Chapter 9, we move on to consider some of the ways in which this is already being addressed in relation to the future development of social work.

putting it into practice

1 What kinds of contact have you had recently with health and/or social care services – as a patient, a carer or a friend or relative? What have been the best points and the worst ones?

2 The language of 'modernisation' in public services emphasises the need for more collaboration and better communication across the boundaries between social work, health care, education and other agencies. What are the obstacles to achieving this, in your view?

3 How should an individual social worker's performance be assessed? What role (if any) should clients have in these assessments?

Further reading

Davies, C., Finlay, L. and Bullman, A. (eds) 2000) *Changing Practice in Health and Social Care*. London: Sage.

Malone, C., Forbat, L., Robb, M. and Seden, J. (2005) *Relating Experience: Stories from Health and Social Care*.

Robb, M., Barrett, S., Komaromy, C. and Rogers, A. (2004) *Communication, Relationships and Care*. London: Routledge/ Open University.

These three edited collections each provide a mix of insights and disciplinary starting-points. The contents range from overviews of policy developments and theoretical debates to intensely personal stories. Taken together, they offer challenging questions as well as useful summaries and comparisons.

9 | The future of psychology and social work

Introduction

In recent years there has been a great deal of flux and change within three domains of the interface between applied psychology and social work in the UK:

- The *intellectual domain*: areas such as child development, domestic violence and mental health have been 'claimed' both by psychology and by social work as disciplines, in terms of formulating theory and carrying out new research; sometimes there is collaboration, but there have also been both divergence and tension.
- The *policy domain*: there are new developments in a number of areas – including professional ethics and governance, user–professional relationships and the research–practice relationship – and these are reshaping the ways in which both psychologists and social workers operate.
- The *organisational domain*: with an increasing push from government for inter-professional and inter-agency collaboration, there have been major changes within and between agencies delivering services, and also in arrangements for training, funding, regulation and inspection. Again, these changes are affecting the ways in which social workers and psychologists regard each other and view opportunities for collaboration at practice level, and also in relation to research initiatives.

There is bound to be continuing change in terms of particular policies, new forms of organisation and specific issues and concerns. In this brief final chapter, we are not aiming to present an exhaustive picture, since many specific details will quickly become outdated. (Despite the fact that each new government finds it opportune to describe public services as 'resistant to change', health and social care organisations have experienced almost continuous waves of major change since the 1970s. What this apparent obsession with 'change' may mean is another debate in itself!) However, we do suggest here that some enduring themes can be identified within recent developments, and that these will continue to inform dialogue and collaboration between social work and applied psychology. The two major themes to which we draw attention below are:

1. Concerns with the relationship between knowledge, risk and practice.
2. Concerns with relationships between disciplines, agencies and professions.

Knowledge, risk and practice

In earlier chapters, we have drawn attention both to the impact of high-profile tragedies (such as child deaths) on social work policy and practice, and to the difference between basing a decision on evidence from psychology or other sources and working from 'intuition' or anecdotal observation. There is a long history of government and professional concern with ensuring that social workers do draw on research, both to ensure high-quality services, and also to minimise the risks of poor practice. While there is a credible argument that we should be aiming to understand and cope with risk in cultural terms, resisting the temptation to think we can eliminate it (Scourfield and Welsh, 2003), this is no reason for evading issues about how best to inform and develop 'critical practice' (Brechin et al., 2000).

In 1980, for example, the Department of Health and Social Security (DHSS) identified the need for systematic research in areas such as the specific skills required in different settings, or the implementation of case review systems (DHSS, 1980). A response from a British Association of Social Workers officer at the time made a strong case for social researchers:

> To engage practitioners in acquiring skills, research skills, even if crude ... to inform their role both as practitioners and as social reformers.
> Etherington, 1984: 26

A generation later, the language of social reform has given way to more cautious and less overtly political terms: 'best value', effectiveness, partnership and user-involvement (DoH, 1998, 2000a, 2000b). However, many of the debates and concerns remain recognisable ones. Periodic surveys have continued to find that, although social workers regularly express a willingness to use research findings, a minority routinely read published research from any discipline; resources to support practitioner access to research findings, or training in research methods, are very limited; most social care research continues to be funded by the Department of Health rather than by local authority social services agencies (Iwaniec and Pinkerton, 1998; Shaw *et al.*, 2003; Owen and Cooke, 2004). Meanwhile, there has been an increasing government preoccupation with identifying 'what works' in public services (Davies *et al.*, 2000), which has sometimes contributed to simplistic forms of 'management by target'.

In this context, two somewhat contrasting responses have emerged. Initiatives in 'evidence-based practice' include advocates for both 'experimental' and 'pragmatic' models (Trinder, 2000; Webb, 2001, 2002). The former have developed explicit comparisons with health research models, questioning the established emphasis on qualitative research in social care and proposing a move towards systematic review skills and experimental methods (see for example Macdonald (1997) and Sheldon and MacDonald (1999)). Organisations such as the Centre for Evidence-Based Social Services (CEBSS) at Exeter University now offer a wide range of training and other resources which draw on this overall approach, and which have strong parallels with older health services research initiatives.

The latter, however – the 'pragmatists' – prefer an assertive emphasis on pluralism in research methods, arguing that many important research questions, particularly those relating to services in the community, require a more sensitive and contextualised approach to gathering and assessing research evidence (see, for example, Shaw and Shaw (1997) and Webb (2001)). Organisations such as 'Making Research Count' have supported researcher–practitioner collaboration in this vein, advancing the notion of 'knowledge-based practice'. This 'conceives of a triangle of research, practitioner wisdom and service user perspectives underpinning the development of practice in social work and social care' (Humphreys *et al.*, 2003: 41).

At government level, the Social Care Institute for Excellence (SCIE) opted for a similarly pragmatic emphasis (SCIE, 2003). Rather than operating with the single hierarchy of evidence that dominates in much health care research, SCIE has developed a framework for describing and reviewing knowledge derived from academic research, practitioners, agencies, users and policy sources. Similarly, the Social Services Inspectorate's annual report for 2002–3 noted that:

> The evidence shows that the services which are most effective, are those where frontline social workers are supported in a clear managerial framework and where they are encouraged to develop 'reflective practice', improving their professional skill in making judgements in very complex situations. *The Victoria Climbié Inquiry Report* notes that 'practice should be governed by *professional judgement* not by rules and procedures'
>
> SSI, 2003: 35 – emphasis in original

This brings us directly to matters of management and organisation, and to the key issues of collaboration between disciplines, agencies and professionals.

Relationships between disciplines, agencies and professions

Psychologists have been determined to (re-)claim some of the ground over which social workers have held sovereignty in the past – for instance, domestic violence, sexual abuse and a range of issues of interest to the new breed of 'counselling psychologists', such as family therapy, grief counselling and so on. Conversely, some writers (e.g. Howe, 1987) appear to have leapfrogged from principles of nineteenth-century behaviourism to modern social work theory, ignoring the ways in which psychological research has refined and applied this knowledge.

In our first edition we noted Sutton's (1981) recognition that CCETSW (Central Council for Education and Training in Social Work) required social work students to demonstrate knowledge and understanding of:

(a) social work theories including their practice in work with individuals, groups and communities and in field, residential and day services; and
(b) processes of human development, socialisation and functioning, both normal and deviant, throughout the life cycle, within a multicultural society; the nature of moral behaviour.

However, CCETSW did not present these theories as psychological or derived from psychology; the implicit assumption was that they were an intrinsic part of social work practice and theory. From both sides, then, there have been indications of unclear boundaries, compounded by both professions being engaged in a protracted process of reflection and self-scrutiny.

In the early years of the 21st century, new social work regulatory and training bodies were established to provide accreditation and accountability: the General Social Care Council to ensure registration of social workers and a move towards social work becoming a graduate profession; the Training Organisation for Personal Social Services to define competences and qualification pathways for social care staff; the Commission for Social Care Inspection to define service standards, and to register and inspect services; the Social Care Institute for Excellence to promote the knowledge base.

However, commentators (including SCIE's own first chief executive) have expressed concern that all these developments are subject to the vagaries of politics, concluding that maintaining strong professional associations is likely to be the best way to sustain and advance the discipline in the long term, and arguing for a 'standing conference' to provide a network for organisations championing social care and social work and its knowledge and competence base (Jones, 2004).

Psychology in Britain, for its part (following the USA), engaged in a study of the future of the psychological sciences (BPS, 1988) and in a study of the future of professional psychology. The BPS now maintains a register of chartered psychologists which secures professional boundaries and provides more control over membership and psychological practice. It is here that distinctions are drawn between professionals with psychology degrees (some of whom are engaged in activities such as family support, stress management and counselling) and those with post-graduate qualifications in psychology who may become chartered psychologists.

At the same time, radical changes have been set in motion in terms of the settings and the organisations in which both social workers and many psychologists (both chartered and non-chartered) work. The Social Services Departments established over 30 years ago are beginning to be eclipsed by new organisations, as we note below. It will take some time for these new working arrangements to crystallise across the UK, particularly since devolution has brought a degree of divergence in structures in Scotland, England and Wales. However, even as specific structures continue to evolve, these will continue to be contexts in which different professionals will collaborate far more closely than in the past, and in which established boundaries may be questioned and renegotiated (Hudson, 2002).

For example, some aspects of established professional territory have been taken on by staff who may not have professional qualifications: the roles of 'personal adviser' and 'family support worker' for example, which have emerged in the early years of the 21st century in government programmes to support parents, operate as 'adjuncts' to professional social workers, nursery teachers or health visitors. In organisational terms, the Primary Care Trusts established from 2002 onwards began to bring together multidisciplinary teams in areas such as mental health and services for older people; pilot versions of Children's Trusts, initiated from 2004 onwards, have been designed to bring together the whole range of services for children, in terms of education, health and social care (DfES, 2004). The momentum for the latter, in particular, has been increased by the findings of Lord Laming's report into the death of Victoria Climbié in 2000, emphasising the disastrous effects of a lack of communication across professions and agencies, but also pointing out that this problem was not new:

> The evidence that attracted most attention at Lord Laming's public hearings into the death of Victoria Climbié described systemic failures with casework practice and supervision as well as serious omissions, inconsistencies and errors in the case recording or reporting and in communications within and between agencies. As a result, information on Victoria observed at first hand by social services, NHS, police and others was not acted on... These themes echo the findings of the many child care inquiries tracing back to Maria Colwell in 1974.
> Lingham, 2004

(For a full discussion, see also Parton, 2004.) In an attempt to move away from old 'blame culture' models, future inquiries and investigations will focus on 'system' failures rather than individual ones, and will be led by the NHS National Patient Safety Agency (NPSA) (DoH, 2001a; Lingham, 2004). Once again, this will keep the spotlight firmly on the issue of inter-professional communication and collaboration.

Conclusions

Psychology and social work are unable to operate as 'value-free' or isolated disciplines. As we have explored in earlier chapters, both theory and empirical research have an uncertain relationship with policy and practice: priorities change, ideas about appropriate 'evidence' are challenged and refined (Broad, 1999). This means that professional practitioners need to reach beyond the 'theory', and to explore the origins and context of social work practice itself. To analyse, reflect and continue to practise is often difficult, but as we look ahead to the continuing development of multidisciplinary and multi-professional organisations and networks, it is more important than ever.

putting it into practice

1 Think of a recent occasion when you had to make an important decision or judgement concerning a client, in your professional capacity (whether in practice or while in training or on placement). What sources of information, advice or knowledge did you consult in arriving at your decision? How would you classify these, e.g. published research findings, published guidelines or training materials, informal discussion with colleagues, formal or informal discussion with a user network or organisation?

2 Spend a few minutes thinking about the different sources of knowledge and information available to you to support good practice. What are they? Which ones are easy to access and which ones are not? What would help to make resources easier to access?

3 Think of an issue in social work practice which you consider (from experience so far) to be a priority for further research to support effective practice. For example, identify an issue where there are differences of opinion about best practice, or where little research or evaluation has been done. How might this question be examined, and who by?

Further reading

Brechin, A., Brown, H. and Eby, M. (2000) *Critical Practice in Health and Social Care*. London: Sage.

An edited collection which introduces a wide range of perspectives. Concepts and theoretical debates are presented clearly, and related to very useful case-study examples from policy and practice. The key ideas here will not become outdated, even though policy details will inevitably change.

Parton, N. (2004) 'From Maria Colwell to Victoria Climbié: Reflections on public inquiries into child abuse a generation apart', *Child Abuse Review*, March, 13(2): 80–94.

An excellent overview of the ways in which policy and practice have been shaped by preventable child deaths, and by the inquiries that have followed them.

SCIE (2003) 'Types and quality of knowledge in social care', *Knowledge Review 3*. London: Social Care Institute for Excellence.

A concise and thoughtful overview of the main sources of knowledge which are available to support social work practice, and of the criteria social workers (and others) can use in appraising and comparing them.

References

Ahn, H. and Wampold, B. E. (2001) 'Where oh where are the specific ingredients? A meta analysis of component studies in counselling and psychotherapy', *Journal of Counseling Psychology*, 48: 251–7.

Ainsworth, M.S. (1964) 'Patterns of attachment behaviour shown by the infant in interaction with his mother', *Merril-Palmer Quarterly*, 10: 51–8.

Ainsworth, M.S. (1996) 'Attachments and other affectional bonds across the life cycle', in C.M. Parkes, J. Steveson-Hinde and P. Marris (eds) *Attachment Across the Life Cycle*. London: Routledge.

Alcock, C., Payne, S. and Sullivan, M. (2000) *Introducing Social Policy*. Harlow: Prentice-Hall.

Allen, J. and Brock, S.A. (2000) *Health Care Communication and Personality Type*. London: Routledge.

Allport, G.W. (1961) *Pattern and Growth in Personality*. London: Holt, Rinehart & Winston.

Anderson, M. (ed.) (1982) *Sociology of the Family*. Harmondsworth: Penguin.

Anderson, J. (2000) *Learning and Memory. An Integrated Approach*, 2nd edn. Chichester: Wiley.

APA (American Psychiatric Association) (1994) *Diagnostic and Statistical Manual*, 4th edn. Washington DC: American Psychiatric Association.

Archer, J. (1999) *The Nature of Grief: The Evolutional and Psychology of Reactions to Loss*. London: Routledge.

Ashworth, P.D. (1979) *Social Interaction and Consciousness*. Chichester: Wiley.

Badinter, E. (1980) *The Myth of Motherhood: An Historical View of the Maternal Instinct*. London: Souvenir Press.

Bandura, A. (1971) *Social Learning Theory*. New York: General Learning Press.

Barclay Report (1982) 'The role and tasks of social workers'. London: NISW.

Barnes, M. (1999) 'Users as citizens: collective action and the local governance of welfare', *Social Policy & Administration*, 33(1): 73–90.

Barnes, M. (2002) 'Bringing difference into deliberation? Disabled people, survivors and local governance', *Policy & Politics*, 30(3): 319–31.

Baron, R.A. and Byrne, D. (2004) *Social Psychology*, 10th edn. London: Allyn & Bacon.

Baron, R.S. and Kerr, N.L. (2003) *Group Process, Group Decision and Group Action*. Buckingham: Open University Press.

Baron-Cohen, S. (2004) *The Essential Difference*. Harmondsworth: Penguin.

Barton, R. (1976) *Institutional Neurosis.* Bristol: J. Wright.

Bayne, R. (1995) *The Myers-Briggs Type Indicator. A Critical Review and Practical Guide.* Cheltenham: Nelson Thornes.

Bayne, R. (2004) *Psychological Types at Work. An MBTI Perspective.* London: Thomson.

Bayne, R. (2005) *Ideas and Evidence: Critical Reflections on MBTI Theory and Practice.* Gainesville, FL: Center for Applications of Psychological Type.

Bayne, R., Horton, I., Merry, T., Noyes, E., and McMahon, G. (1999) *The Counsellor's Handbook,* 2nd edn. Cheltenham: Nelson Thornes.

Belsky, J. (1999) *The Psychology of Ageing: Theory, Research and Interventions.* Pacific Grove, CA: Brooks-Cole.

Belsky, J. (2001). 'Developmental Risks (Still) Associated with Early Child Care', *Journal of Child Psychology and Psychiatry,* 42: 845–59.

Benson, H. (1977) *The Relaxation Response.* London: Collins Fontana Paperbacks.

Beresford, P. and Croft, S. (2001) 'Service users' knowledges and the social construction of social work', *Journal of Social Work,* 1(3): 295–316.

Berger, P. (1966) 'Identity as a problem of knowledge', *Archives European de Sociologie,* 7: 105–15.

Berger, P. and Kellner, H. (1964/1982) 'Marriage and the construction of reality', in M. Anderson (ed.) *Sociology of the Family.* Harmondsworth: Penguin.

Bettelheim, B. (1979) *The Informed Heart: Autonomy in a Mass Age.* New York: Avon.

Bion, W.R. (1961) *Experiences in Groups.* London: Tavistock.

Bolton, G., Howlett, S., Lago, C. and Wright, J.K. (eds) (2004) *Writing Cures. An Introductory Handbook of Writing in Counselling and Therapy.* Hove: Brunner-Routledge.

Bond, M. (1986) *Stress and Self-awareness: A Guide for Nurses.* Oxford: Heinemann.

Bond, T. (2000) *Standards and Ethics for Counselling in Action,* 2nd edn. London: Sage.

Boon, J., Davies, G.W. and Noon, E. (1993) 'Children in court', in R. Bayne and P. Nicolson (eds) *Counselling and Psychology for Health Professionals,* London: Chapman & Hall.

Boul, L. A. (2003) 'Men's health and middle age', *Sexualities, Evolution and Gender,* 5(1): 5–22.

Bowlby, J. (1951) *Maternal Care and Mental Health.* Geneva, World Health Organisation/New York: Shocken Books.

Bowlby, J. (1969/1982) *Attachment and Loss, Volume 1.* New York: Basic Books.

Bowlby, J. (1980) *Attachment and Loss, Volume 3.* New York: Basic Books.

BPS (British Psychological Society) (1988) *The Future of the Psychological Sciences,* paper prepared by the Scientific Affairs Board of the BPS, Leicester.

Breakwell, G. (1997) *Facing Physical Violence.* Oxford: Blackwell.

Brechin, A., Brown, H. and Eby, M. (2000) *Critical Practice in Health and Social Care.* London: Sage.

Brems, C. (2001) *Basic Skills in Psychotherapy and Counselling*. London: Brooks/Cole.

Broad, B. (ed) (1999) *The Politics of Social Work Research and Evaluation*. Venture Press in association with The Social Work Research Association, available from BASW, http://www.basw.co.uk.

Brown, A. (1979) *Groupwork*. London: Heinemann.

Burr, J.A. and Nicolson, P. (2004) *Researching Health Care Consumers: Critical Approaches*. Basingstoke: Palgrave Macmillan.

Campbell, A. (2002) *A Mind of Her Own: The Evolutionary Psychology of Women*. Oxford: Oxford University Press.

Cardonna, F. (1994) 'Facing an uncertain future', in A. Obholzer and V. Zagier Roberts (eds) *The Unconscious at Work: Individual and Organisational Stress in the Human Services*. London: Routledge.

Carr, S. (1997) *Type Clarification. Finding the Fit*. Oxford: OPP.

Cartwright, D. and Zander, A. (1968) (eds) *Group Dynamics: Research and Theory*. New York: Harper & Row.

CCETSW (1967) 'Human growth and behaviour as a subject of study for social workers', CCETSW Discussion Paper no. 2.

CCETSW (1988) 'The qualifying diploma in social work', CCETSW Paper 20, 9 February.

Clegg, F. (1988) 'Disasters: Can psychologists help the survivors?', *The Psychologist*, 1(): 134–5.

Clulow, C. (1994) 'Balancing care and control: the supervisory relationship as a focus for promoting organisational health', in A. Obholzer and V. Zagier Roberts (eds) *The Unconscious at Work: Individual and Organisational Stress in the Human Services*. London: Routledge.

Cochrane, A. and Clarke, J. (1993) *Comparing Welfare States: Britain in International Context*. London: Sage.

Cohen, S. and Taylor, L. (1972) *Psychological Survival*. Harmondsworth: Penguin.

Cooper, C.L., Dewe, P.J. and O'Driscoll, M.P. (2001) *Organizational Stress: A Review and Critique of Theory, Research and Applications*. London: Sage.

Currer, C. (2001) *Responding to Grief: Dying, Bereavement and Social Care*. Basingstoke: Palgrave Macmillan.

Curtis Committee, (1946) *Report of the Care of Children Committee*, HMSO.

Davenport, D.S. and Pipes, R.B. (1990) *Introduction to Psychotherapy: Common Clinical Wisdom*. London: Prentice Hall.

Davies, C. (2000) 'Frameworks for regulation and accountability: threat or opportunity?', in A. Brechin, H. Brown and M. Eby (eds) *Critical Practice in Health and Social Care*. London: Sage.

Davies, G.M. (1988) 'The use of video in child abuse trials', *The Psychologist: Bulletin of the British Psychological Society*, 1: 20–2.

Davies, H., Nutley, S. and Smith, P. (eds) (2000) *What Works? Evidence-based Policy and Practice in Public Services*. Bristol: Policy Press.

DfES (Department for Education and Skills) (2004) *Every Child Matters: Next Steps*. Nottingham: DfES.

DHSS (Department of Health and Social Security) (1980) 'Directions for research in social work and the social services, 1980. A working party report to the DHSS Research Liaison Group for Local Authority Social Services'. London: DHSS.

Dickson, A. (1982) *A Woman in Your Own Right*. London: Quartet Books.

Dinnerstein, D. (1976) *The Rocking of the Cradle and the Ruling of the World*. New York: Harper & Row.

DiTiberio, J.K. and Hammer, A.L. (1993) *Introduction to Type in College*. Palo Alto, CA: Consulting Psychologists Press.

Dodd, N. and Bayne, R. (in press) 'Psychological type and choice of counselling model by experienced counsellors', *Journal of Psychological Type*.

DoH (Department of Health) (1998) *Modernising Social Services: Promoting Independence, Improving Protection, Raising Standards*. London: Stationery Office.

DoH (Department of Health) (2000a) *A Quality Strategy for Social Care*. London: DoH.

DoH (Department of Health) (2000b) *Research and Development for a First Class Service*. Leeds: Department of Health.

DoH (Department of Health) (2001a) *Treatment Choice in Psychological Therapies in Counselling*. London: DoH.

DoH (Department of Health) (2001b) *An Organisation With A Memory*. London: DoH.

Douglas, J.W.B. and Blomfield, J.M. (1958) *Children Under Five*. London: Allen & Unwin.

Douglas, T. (1978) *Basic Groupwork*. London: Tavistock.

Dovidio, J.F., Glick, P. and Rudman, L.A. (2005) (eds) *On the Nature of Prejudice: Fifty Years after Allport*. Oxford: Blackwell Publishing.

Dryden, W. and Feltham, C. (1992) *Brief Counselling*. Maidenhead: Open University Press.

Dryden, W. and Feltham, C. (in press) *Brief Counselling*, 2nd edn. Maidenhead: Open University Press.

Dunning, D. (2003) *Introduction to Type and Communication*. Palo Alto, CA: Consulting Psychologists Press.

Eby, M. (2000) 'Understanding professional development', in Brechin *et al.* (eds) *Critical Practice in Health and Social Care*. London: Sage/Open University.

Eckerman, C.O. and Whatley, J.L. (1977) 'Toys and social interaction between infant peers', *Child Development*, 48: 1645–56.

Egan, G. (2002) *The Skilled Helper*, 7th edn. Pacific Grove, CA: Brooks/Cole.

Ehlers, A., Mayou, R.A. and Bryant, B. (2003) 'Cognitive predictors of posttraumatic stress disorder in children: results of a prospective longitudinal study', *Behaviour Research and Therapy*, 41: 1–10.

Ekman, P. and Friesen, W.V. (1975) *Unmasking the Face*. London: Prentice Hall.

Epstein, S. (1979) 'The stability of behavior: I. On predicting most of the people much of the time', *Journal of Personality and Social Psychology*, 37: 1097–126.

Erikson, E.H. (1968) *Childhood and Society*. New York: Norton.

Etherington, S. (1984) 'Social research and social work practice', *Research, Policy and Planning*, 2(1): 25–7.

Evison, R. and Horobin, R. (2005) Co-counselling', in C. Feltham and I. Horton (eds) *Handbook of Counselling and Psychotherapy*, 2nd edn. London: Sage.

Feltham, C. and Horton, I. (eds) (2006) *Handbook of Counselling and Psychotherapy*, 2nd edn. London: Sage.

Ferlie, E., Ashburner, L. and Pettigrew, A. (1996) *The New Public Management in Action*.

Festinger, J.R.P. and Raven, B.H. (1959) *Social Pressures in Informal Groups: A Study of a Housing Community*. London: Harper & Row.

Fineman, S. (1993) *Emotion in Organisations*. London: Sage.

Fitzsimmons, S. (1999) *Type and Time Management*. Edmonton: Psychometrics Canada Ltd.

French, J.R.P. and Raven, B.H. (1959) 'The bases of social power', in D. Cartwright, *Studies in Social Power*. Ann Arbor, MI: University of Michigan Press.

Freud, S. (1922) *Group Psychology and the Analysis of the Ego*. London: Hogarth.

Freud, S. (1949) *An Outline of Psychoanalysis*. New York: Norton.

Funder, D.C. (1995) 'On the accuracy of personality judgement: A realistic approach', *Psychological Review*, 102:, 652–70.

Funder, D.C. (2001) 'Personality', *Annual Review of Psychology*, 52: 197–221.

Furnham, A. and Schofield, S. (1987) 'Accepting personality test feedback: A review of the Barnum effect', *Current Psychology Research and Reviews*, 6: 162–78.

Gannon, L.R. (1992) 'Sexuality and the menopause', in P.Y.L. Choi and P. Nicolson (eds) *Female Sexuality: Psychology, Biology and Social Context*. Brighton: Harvester.

Gannon, L.R. (1999) *Women and Ageing: Transcending the Myths*. London: Routledge.

Garfinkel, M. (1967) *Studies in Ethnomethodology*. Englewood Cliffs, NJ: Prentice Hall.

Gendlin, E.T. (1981) *Focusing*, 2nd edn. London: Bantam.

Gerber, I. *et al.* (1975) 'Brief therapy to the aged and bereaved' in B. Shoenberg *et al.* (eds) *Bereavement: Its Psychosocial Aspects*. New York: Columbia University Press.

Gibbs, D. (1999) 'Disabled people and the research community', paper presented to the ESRC Seminar Series 'Theorising social work research: Who owns the research process?', Belfast, 20.9.99. Available electronically at http://www.elsc.org.uk.socialcareresource/tswr/seminar2/gibbs.htm.

Gilligan, C. (1982/1993) *In a Different Voice: Psychological Theory and Women's Development*. London: Harvard University Press.

Gilmore, S.K. (1973) *The Counselor-in-Training*. London: Prentice Hall.

Glassop, L.I. (2002) 'The organisational benefits of teams', *Human Relations*, 55(2): 225–49.

Goffman, E. (1968) *Asylums*. Harmondsworth: Penguin.

Gomm, R. and Davies, C. (2000) *Using Evidence in Health and Social Care*. London: Sage.

Gott, M. (2005) *Sexuality, Sexual Health and Ageing*. Maidenhead: McGraw-Hill.

Gough, B. and McFadden, M. (2001) *Critical Social Psychology: An Introduction*. Basingstoke: Palgrave Macmillan.

Greenberg, L.S. and Dompierre, L.M. (1981) 'Specific effects of Gestalt two-chair dialogue on intrapsychic conflict in counselling', *Journal of Counseling Psychology*, 28(4): 288–94.

Griffiths, R. (1988) *Community Care: Agenda for Action*. DHSS.

Harlow, H.F. (1961) The development of affectional patterns in infant monkeys', in B.M. Foss (ed.) *Determinants of Infant Behaviour*. New York: International Universities Press.

Harré, R. and Secord, P.F. (1972) *The Exploration of Social Behaviour*. Oxford: Blackwell.

Harris, T. and Bifulco, A. (1996) 'Loss of parent in childhood, attachment style and depression in adulthood', in C.M. Parkes, J. Steveson-Hinde and P. Marris (eds) *Attachment Across the Life Cycle*. London: Routledge.

Hartup, W.W. (1970) 'Peer interaction and social organisation', in P.H. Mussen (ed.) *Carmichael's Manual of Child Psychology*. New York: Wiley.

Harvey, P. (1988) *Health Psychology*. London: Longman.

Herzog, A.R., Rodgers, W.L. and Woodworth, J. (1982) 'Subjective well-being among different age groups'. Research Report No. 9107. Ann Arbor: University of Michigan, Institute of Social Research.

Herzog, C. (1996) 'Research design in studies of ageing and cognition', in J.E. Birren and K.W. Schaie (eds) *A Handbook of the Psychology of Aging*. New York: Academic Press.

Hill, C.E. (2004) *Helping Skills. Facilitating Exploration, Insight and Action*, 2nd edn. Washington, DC: APA.

Holland, C.A. (1995) 'Ageing Memory', in F. Glendenning and I.A. Stuart-Hamilton (eds) *Psychology: Changes in Old Age*. Avebury Press.

Holland, C.A., Rabbitt, P. *et al.* (1996) 'A cross-sectional examination of effects of depression, age, gender, and socio-economic group cognitive performance. Do previously found relationships differ when a depression inventory especially designed for use with older people is employed?', *Facts and Research in Gerontology*, 1–14.

Holloway, E. (1995) *Clinical Supervision: A Systems Approach*. London: Sage.

Howe, D. (1987) *An Introduction to Social Work Theory*. Aldershot: Wildwood House.

Hubble, M.A., Duncan, B.I. and Miller, S.D. (eds) (1999) *The Heart and Soul of Change. What Works in Therapy?*. Washington, DC: APA.

Hudson, B. (2000) 'Social services and primary care groups: A window of collaborative opportunity?', *Health and Social Care in the Community*, 8(4): 242–50.

Hudson, B. (2002) 'Interprofessionality in health and social care: the Achilles' heel of partnership?', *Journal of Interprofessional Care*, 16(1): 7–17.

Hudson, B.L. and Macdonald, G.M. (1986) *Behavioural Social Work: An Introduction*. London: Macmillan – now Basingstoke: Palgrave Macmillan.

t, bonding ~nd psychiatric pr~ after
C.M. Parkes,~ Stevenson-Hi~and P.
s the Life Cycle. ~don: Routle~.
ses. London: Rout~
Colwell to Victoria Cli~
se a generation apart', Chil~ ~ons on
~ Review,
~ms. London: Macmillan – now Basing~ ~e:

~d Sharp, L.K. (1990) 'Accelerating the coping
~y and Social Psychology, 58: 528–37.
~ogy and social pathology', in J.E. Birren and
~ of the Psychology of Ageing. New York:

~lgement of the Child. New York: Free Press.
~ Family. London: Faber & Faber.
~ons of the Myers-Briggs Type Indicator in
~d edn. Gainesville, FL: Centre for Application

~d Majors, M.S. (2001) MBTI Step II Manual.
~sychologists Press.
~ary. New York: St. Martin's Press.
~iary. London: Angus & Robertson.
~Behaviour: Theory, Research and Training.

~ive intervention with the recently bereaved',
~ogy, 34: 1450–4.
~ve function of the therapist', in D. Wexler and
~in Client-Centred Therapy. New York: Wiley.
~1986) Children of Social Worlds. Cambridge:

~P. (1972) Social Work Education in Conflict.

~ion in mothers of pre-school children', Journal
~sychiatry, 17: 25–78.
~cal Research. Milton Keynes: Open University

~ Becoming a Person: A Therapists View of
~onstable.
~ an unappreciated way of being', in C. Rogers,
~oughton Mifflin.
~ts on the issue of equality in psychotherapy',
~chology, 27: 38–40.
~2000) Alas Poor Darwin: Arguments against
~London: Jonathan Cape.
~othe the savage breast', Behaviour Research and

Hughes, M. et al. (1980) Nurseries Now. Harmondsworth: Penguin.
Humphreys, C., Berridge, D., Butler, I. and Ruddick, R. (2003) 'Making research count: The development of 'knowledge-based practice', Research, Policy and Planning, 21(1): 41–9.
Iwaniec, D. and Pinkerton, J. (1998) Making Research Work: Promoting Child Care Policy and Practice. Chichester: Wiley.
Janis, I.L. (1972) Victims of Groupthink: A Psychological Study of Foreign Policy Decision and Fiascos. Boston: Houghton Mifflin.
Jaques, E. (1955) 'Social systems as a defence against persecutory and depressive anxiety', in M. Klein et al. (eds) New Directions in Psycho-analysis. London: Tavistock.
Jones, F. and Bright, J. (2001) Stress: Myth, Theory and Research. London: Prentice Hall.
Jones, M. (1968) Social Psychiatry in Practice. Harmondsworth: Penguin.
Jones, R. (2004) 'Death of the department', Community Care, 8 July.
Keirsey, D. (1998) Please Understand Me II. Del Mar, CA: Prometheus Nemesis.
Kennedy-Moore, E. and Watson, J.C. (1999) Expressing Emotion: Myths, Realities and Therapeutic Strategies. London Guilford Press.
Kenniston, K. (1977) All Our Children: The American Family Under Pressure. New York: Harcourt.
Kenrick, D.T. and Funder, D.C. (1988) 'Profiting from controversy: lessons from the person-situation debate', American Psychologist, 43:, 23–34.
Kincey, V. (1974) 'The Evaluation of a bereavement counselling service', MSc Thesis, University of Manchester.
Kipnis, D. (2001) 'Using power: Newtons's second law', in A.Y. Lee-chai and J.A. Bargh (eds) The Use and Abuse of Power: Multiple Perspectives on the Causes of Corruption. London: Psychology Press.
Klaus, H.M. and Kennell, J.M. (1976) Maternal Infant Bonding. St Louis, MI: Mosby.
Kohlberg, L. (1969) 'Stage and sequence: The cognitive-developmental approach to socialisation', in D.A. Goslin (ed.) Handbook of Socialisation Theory and Research. Chicago: Rand McNally.
Kohlberg, L. (1976) 'Moral stages and moralisation: The cognitive-developmental approach', in T. Lickona (ed.) Moral Developent and Behaviour. New York: Holt, Rinehart & Winston.
Kolb, D.M. and Bartunek, J.M. (1992) Hidden Conflict in Organisations. London: Sage.
Konopka, G. (1963) Social Groupwork: A Helping Process, Englewood Cliffs, NJ: Prentice-Hall.
Kosslyn, S.M. and Rosenberg, R.S. (2004) Psychology. The Brain, The Person, The World, 2nd edn. London: Allyn & Bacon.
La Fontaine, J. (1989) 'Child sexual abuse: an ESRC research briefing', After Abuse. British Agencies for Adoption and Fostering.
Ladyman, S. (2004) Speech to the GSCC 3rd Annual Conference at the QEII Conference Centre. www.dh.gov.uk/NewsHome/Speeches/SpeechesList/SpeechesArticle/fsen?CO.
Laing, R.D. (1969) Self and Others. Harmondsworth: Penguin.

Lawrence, G. (1997) *Looking at Type and Learning Styles*. Gainsville, FL: Center for Applications of Psychological Type.

Lazarus, A.A. and Mayne, T.J. (1990 'Relaxation: some limitations, side effects, and proposed solutions', *Psychotherapy*, 27: 261–6.

Lee, P. and Pithers, D. (1980) 'Radical residential child care: Trojan horse or non-runner', in M. Brake and R. Bailey (eds) *Radical Social Work and Practice*. London: Arnold.

Ley, P. (1988) *Communicating with Patients*. London: Croom Helm.

Linder, R. (2000) *What Will I do With my Money? How your Personality Affects your Financial Behaviour*. Chicago, IL: Northfield.

Lingham, A. (2004) 'An end to the blame game?', *Community Care*, 11 March.

Linton, R. (1949) *The Study of Man*. New York: Appleton-Century-Croft.

Lord, C.G., Lepper, M.R. and Preston, E. (1984) 'Considering the opposite: a corrective strategy for social judgement', *Journal of Personality and Social Psychology*, 47:, 1231–43.

Maas, M. (1980) 'Research and knowledge base', in *Discovery and Development in Social Work Education*. Vienna: International Association of Schools SW Publications.

Macdonald, G. (1997) 'Social Work Research: the State We're In', *Journal of Interprofessional Care*, 11(1): 57–65.

Maguire, P. (1981) 'Doctor–patient skills', in M. Argyle (ed.) *Social Skills and Health*. London: Methuen.

Marris, P. (1986) *Loss and Change*. London: Tavistock.

Marris, P. (1996) 'The social construction of uncertainty', in C.M. Parkes, J. Steveson-Hinde and P. Marris (eds) *Attachment Across the Life Cycle*. London: Routledge.

Martin, D. (1962) *Adventure in Psychiatry*. London: Cassirer.

McDougall, W. (1922) *The Group Mind*. Cambridge: Cambridge University Press.

McLeod, J. (2003) *An Introduction to Counselling*, 3rd edn. Buckingham: Open University Press.

Mead, G.H. (1934/1967) *Mind, Self, and Society*. Chicago: University of Chicago Press.

Menzies, I.E.P. (1970) *The Functioning of Social Systems as a Defence against Anxiety*. London: Tavistock Institute of Human Relations.

Menzies Lyth, I.E.P. (1992) *Containing Anxiety in Institutions, Selected essays, Volume 1*. London: Free Association Press.

Merry, T. (2002) *Learning Person-Centred Counselling*, 2nd edn. Ross-on-Wye: PCCS Books.

Milgram, S. (1974) *Obedience to Authority*. New York: Harper & Row.

Miller, E.J. and Gwynne, G.V. (1972) *A Life Apart*. London: Tavistock.

Mills, C.K. and Wooster, A.D. (1987) 'Crying in the counselling situation', *British Journal of Guidance and Counselling*, 15: 125–30.

Mitchell, J. (2000) *Mad Men and Medusas: Reclaiming Hysteria and the Effects of Sibling Relations on the Human Condition*. Harmondsworth: Penguin.

Parkes, C.M. (1996) 'Attachmer bereavement in adult life', in Marris (eds) *Attachment Acro*

Parry, G. (1990) *Coping with C*

Parton, N. (2004) 'From Maria public inquiries into child abu 13(2): 80–94.

Payne, M. (1982) *Working in Te* Palgrave Macmillan.

Pennebaker, J.W., Colder, M. an process', *Journal of Personali*

Pfeiffer, E. (1977) 'Psychopatho K.W. Schaie (eds) *Handboo* Academic Press.

Piaget, J. (1932) *The Moral Ju*

Pincus, L. (1976) *Death and the*

Provost, J.A. (1993) *Applicati Counselling: A Casebook*, 2n of Psychological Type.

Quenk, N.L., Hammer, A.L. a Palo Alto, CA: Consulting P

Rainer, T. (1978) *The New D*

Rainer, T. (1980) *The New D*

Rakos, R. (1991) *Assertive* London: Routledge.

Raphael, B. (1977) 'Preventa *Archives of General Psycho*

Rice, L.N. (1974) 'The evocat L.N. Rice (eds) *Innovation*

Richards, M. and Light, P. (Polity Press.

Richards, M. and Righton, London: NISW Papers.

Richman, N. (1976) 'Depress of Child Psychology and P

Roberts, B. (2000) *Biographi* Press.

Rogers, C. (1961/2002) *On Psychotherapy*. London: C

Rogers, C. (1975) 'Empathio *A Way of Being*. Boston:

Rogers, C. (1987) 'Comme *Journal of Humanistic Ps*

Rose, H. and Rose, S. (*Evolutionary Psychology*.

Rosenthal, T. (1993) 'To s *Therapy*, 31(5): 439–62.

Rutter, M. (1972) *Maternal Deprivation Reassessed*. Harmondsworth: Penguin Education.

Rutter, M. (1989) 'Pathways from childhood to adult life', *Journal of Child Psychology and Psychiatry*, 30 (1), pp. 23–51.

Rutter, M. (2000) 'Children in substitute care: Some conceptual considerations and research implications', *Children and Youth Services Review*, 22(9/10): 685–703.

Sapolsky, R.M. (1998) *Why Zebras Don't Get Ulcers. An Updated Guide to Stress, Stress-related Diseases and Coping*. Basingstoke: Macmillan – now Palgrave Macmillan.

Sayers, J. (1982) *Biological Politics*. London: Tavistock.

Scarr, S. and Dunn, J. (1987) *Mother Care/Other Care*. Harmondsworth: Penguin.

Schaffer, H.R. and Emmerson, P.E. (1964) *The Development of Social Attachments in Infancy*. Monographs of the Society for Research in Child Development.

Scheflen, A.C. (1964) 'The significance of posture in communication systems', *Psychiatry*, 27: 316–31.

SCIE (Social Care Institute for Excellence) (2003) 'Types and quality of knowledge in social care', *Knowledge Review 3*. London: Socal Care Institute for Excellence.

Scott, W.R. (1992) 'Health care organisations in the 1980s: The convergence of public and professional control systems', in J.W. Meyer and W.R. Scott, *Organisational Environments: Ritual and Rationality*. London: Sage.

Scourfield, J. and Welsh, I. (2003) 'Risk, reflexivity and social control in child protection: new times or same old story?', *Critical Social Policy*, 23(3): 398–420.

Seden, J. (2005) *Counselling Skills in Social Work Practice*, 2nd edn. Maidenhead: Open University Press.

Seebohm Report (1968) *Report of the Committee on Local Authority and Allied Personal Social Services*. HMSO.

Seligman, M.E.P. (1995) *What You Can Change and What You Can't*. New York: Fawcett Columbine.

Shaw, I., Keane, S. and Faulkner, A. (2003) *Practitioner Research in Social Care: A Survey and Case Study Analysis*. Unpublished report, University of York.

Shaw, I. and Shaw, A. (1997) 'Keeping social work honest: Evaluating as profession and practice', *British Journal of Social Work*, 27: 847–69.

Sheldon, B. and MacDonald, G. (1999) *Research and Practice in Social Care: Mind the Gap*. Exeter: Centre for Evidence-Based Social Services.

Sheldon, K.M. and Kasser, T. (2001) 'Goals, congruence and positive well-being: New empirical validation for humanistic ideas', *Journal of Humanistic Psychology*, 41: 30–50.

Skinner, B.F. (1953) *Science and Human Behaviour*. New York: Free Press.

Smail, D. (1987) *Taking Care*. London: Dent.

Smith, C.R. (1982) *Social Work with the Dying and Bereaved*. London: Macmillan – Basingstoke: Palgrave Macmillan.

Smith, J.B. (1993) 'Teachers' grading styles: The languages of thinking and feeling', *Journal of Psychological Type*, 26: 37–41.

Smyth, J.M. (1998) 'Written emotional expression: effect sizes, outcome types, and moderating variables', *Journal of Consulting and Clinical Psychology*, 66: 174–84.

Spera, S.P., Buhrfeind, E.D. and Pennebaker, J.W. (1994) 'Creative writing and coping with job loss', *Academy of Management Journal*, 37: 722–33.

Spitz, R.A. (1945) 'Hospitalisation: an inquiry into the genesis of psychiatric conditions in early childhood', *Psychoanalytic Studies of the Child*, 1: 53–74.

SSI (Social Services Inspectorate) (2003) *SSI Annual Report 2002–2003*.

Stevens, A. (1989) 'The politics of caring', *The Psychologist*, 2(3): 110–10.

Stiles, W.B., Shapiro, D.A. and Elliott, R. (1986) 'Are all psychotherapies equivalent?', *American Psychologist*, 41:, 165–80.

Sue, D.W. and Sue, D. (1990) *Counseling the Culturally Different: Theory and Practice*, 2nd edn. Chichester: Wiley.

Sutton, C. (1981) *Social Work, Community Work and Psychology*. Oxford: Blackwell.

Sylva, K. *et al.* (2003) *The Effective Provision of Pre-School Education Project*. Institute of Education, University of London.

Tallman, K. and Bohart, A.C. (1999) 'The client as a common factor: Clients as self-healers', in M.A. Hubble *et al.* (eds) *The Heart and Soul of Change*. Washington, DC: American Psychological Association.

Tieger, P.D. and Barron-Tieger, B. (2001) *Do What You Are*, 3rd edn. London: Little, Brown.

Tilbury, C. (2004) 'The influence of performance measurement on child welfare policy and practice', *British Journal of Social Work*, 34: 225–241.

Tizard, B. (1975) *Adoption: A Second Chance*. London: Open Books.

Trinder, L. (ed.) (2000) *Evidence-based Practice: A Critical Appraisal*. Oxford: Blackwell Science.

Tuckman, B.W. (1965) 'Developmental sequence in small groups', *Psychological Bulletin*, 63(6): 384–99.

Turney, D. and Tanner, K. (2001) 'Working with neglected children and their families', *Journal of Social Work Practice* 15(2): 193–204.

Twelvetrees, A. (1982) *Community Work*. London: Macmillan – now Basingstoke: Palgrave Macmillan.

Ussher, J.M. (2006) *Managing the Monstrous Feminine* London: Taylor & Francis.

VanSant, S. (2003) *Wired for Conflict*. Gainesville, FL: Center for Application of Psychological Type.

Webb, S. (2001) 'Some Cconsiderations on the validity of evidence-based practice in social work', *British Journal of Social Work*, 31: 57–80.

Webb, S. (2002) 'Evidence-based practice and decision analysis in social work', *Journal of Social Work*, 2(1): 45–63.

Westcott, H.L. (2003) 'Are children reliable witnesses to their experiences?', in P. Reder, S. Duncan and C. Lucey (eds) *Studies in the Assessment of Parenting*. London: Brunner Routledge.

Westcott, H.L. and Kynan, S. (2004) The application of a "story-telling" framework to investigate interviews for suspected child sexual abuse', *Legal and Criminological Psychology*, 9: 37–56.

Williams, F. (1993) 'Gender, "race" and class in British welfare policy', in A. Cochrane and J. Clarke (eds) *Comparing Welfare States: Britain in International Context*. London: Sage.

Willis, A. and Riciutti, H.N. (1974) *A Good Beginning for Babies: Guidelines for Group Care*. Washington: National Association for the Education of Young Children.

Wilson, A. and Beresford, P. (2000) 'Anti-oppressive practice: Emancipation or appropriation?', *British Journal of Social Work*, 30: 553–73.

Yalom, I.D. (1989) *Love's Executioner and Other Tales of Psychotherapy*. Harmondsworth: Penguin.

Yalom, I.D. (2001) *The Gift of Therapy. Reflections on being a Therapist*. London: Piatkus.

Zagier Roberts, V. (1994) 'The self assigned impossible task', in A. Obholzer and V. Zagier Roberts (eds) *The Unconscious at Work: Individual and Organisational Stress in the Human Services*. London: Routledge.

Zilbergeld, B. (1983) *The Shrinking of America: Myths of Psychological Change*. Boston: Little Brown & Co.

Zimbardo, P. G. *et al.* (1976) *Influencing Attitudes and Changing Behaviour*, 2nd edn. London: Addison-Wesley.

Zoritch, B., Roberts, J. and Oakley, A. (1998) 'The health and welfare effects of day-care: A systematic review of randomised controlled trials', *Social Science & Medicine*, 47(3): 317–28.

Index

Hughes, M. *et al.* (1980) *Nurseries Now.* Harmondsworth: Penguin.

Humphreys, C., Berridge, D., Butler, I. and Ruddick, R. (2003) 'Making research count: The development of 'knowledge-based practice', *Research, Policy and Planning,* 21(1): 41–9.

Iwaniec, D. and Pinkerton, J. (1998) *Making Research Work: Promoting Child Care Policy and Practice.* Chichester: Wiley.

Janis, I.L. (1972) *Victims of Groupthink: A Psychological Study of Foreign Policy Decision and Fiascos.* Boston: Houghton Mifflin.

Jaques, E. (1955) 'Social systems as a defence against persecutory and depressive anxiety', in M. Klein *et al.* (eds) *New Directions in Psychoanalysis.* London: Tavistock.

Jones, F. and Bright, J. (2001) *Stress: Myth, Theory and Research.* London: Prentice Hall.

Jones, M. (1968) *Social Psychiatry in Practice.* Harmondsworth: Penguin.

Jones, R. (2004) 'Death of the department', *Community Care,* 8 July.

Keirsey, D. (1998) *Please Understand Me II.* Del Mar, CA: Prometheus Nemesis.

Kennedy-Moore, E. and Watson, J.C. (1999) *Expressing Emotion: Myths, Realities and Therapeutic Strategies.* London Guilford Press.

Kenniston, K. (1977) *All Our Children: The American Family Under Pressure.* New York: Harcourt.

Kenrick, D.T. and Funder, D.C. (1988) 'Profiting from controversy: lessons from the person-situation debate', *American Psychologist,* 43:, 23–34.

Kincey, V. (1974) 'The Evaluation of a bereavement counselling service', MSc Thesis, University of Manchester.

Kipnis, D. (2001) 'Using power: Newtons's second law', in A.Y. Lee-chai and J.A. Bargh (eds) *The Use and Abuse of Power: Multiple Perspectives on the Causes of Corruption.* London: Psychology Press.

Klaus, H.M. and Kennell, J.M. (1976) *Maternal Infant Bonding.* St Louis, MI: Mosby.

Kohlberg, L. (1969) 'Stage and sequence: The cognitive-developmental approach to socialisation', in D.A. Goslin (ed.) *Handbook of Socialisation Theory and Research.* Chicago: Rand McNally.

Kohlberg, L. (1976) 'Moral stages and moralisation: The cognitive-developmental approach', in T. Lickona (ed.) *Moral Development and Behaviour.* New York: Holt, Rinehart & Winston.

Kolb, D.M. and Bartunek, J.M. (1992) *Hidden Conflict in Organisations.* London: Sage.

Konopka, G. (1963) *Social Groupwork: A Helping Process,* Englewood Cliffs, NJ: Prentice-Hall.

Kosslyn, S.M. and Rosenberg, R.S. (2004) *Psychology. The Brain, The Person, The World,* 2nd edn. London: Allyn & Bacon.

La Fontaine, J. (1989) 'Child sexual abuse: an ESRC research briefing', *After Abuse.* British Agencies for Adoption and Fostering.

Ladyman, S. (2004) Speech to the GSCC 3rd Annual Conference at the QEII Conference Centre. www.dh.gov.uk/NewsHome/Speeches/SpeechesList/SpeechesArticle/fsen?CO.

Laing, R.D. (1969) *Self and Others.* Harmondsworth: Penguin.

Lawrence, G. (1997) *Looking at Type and Learning Styles*. Gainsville, FL: Center for Applications of Psychological Type.

Lazarus, A.A. and Mayne, T.J. (1990 'Relaxation: some limitations, side effects, and proposed solutions', *Psychotherapy*, 27: 261–6.

Lee, P. and Pithers, D. (1980) 'Radical residential child care: Trojan horse or non-runner', in M. Brake and R. Bailey (eds) *Radical Social Work and Practice*. London: Arnold.

Ley, P. (1988) *Communicating with Patients*. London: Croom Helm.

Linder, R. (2000) *What Will I do With my Money? How your Personality Affects your Financial Behaviour*. Chicago, IL: Northfield.

Lingham, A. (2004) 'An end to the blame game?', *Community Care*, 11 March.

Linton, R. (1949) *The Study of Man*. New York: Appleton-Century-Croft.

Lord, C.G., Lepper, M.R. and Preston, E. (1984) 'Considering the opposite: a corrective strategy for social judgement', *Journal of Personality and Social Psychology*, 47:, 1231–43.

Maas, M. (1980) 'Research and knowledge base', in *Discovery and Development in Social Work Education*. Vienna: International Association of Schools SW Publications.

Macdonald, G. (1997) 'Social Work Research: the State We're In', *Journal of Interprofessional Care*, 11(1): 57–65.

Maguire, P. (1981) 'Doctor–patient skills', in M. Argyle (ed.) *Social Skills and Health*. London: Methuen.

Marris, P. (1986) *Loss and Change*. London: Tavistock.

Marris, P. (1996) 'The social construction of uncertainty', in C.M. Parkes, J. Steveson-Hinde and P. Marris (eds) *Attachment Across the Life Cycle*. London: Routledge.

Martin, D. (1962) *Adventure in Psychiatry*. London: Cassirer.

McDougall, W. (1922) *The Group Mind*. Cambridge: Cambridge University Press.

McLeod, J. (2003) *An Introduction to Counselling*, 3rd edn. Buckingham: Open University Press.

Mead, G.H. (1934/1967) *Mind, Self, and Society*. Chicago: University of Chicago Press.

Menzies, I.E.P. (1970) *The Functioning of Social Systems as a Defence against Anxiety*. London: Tavistock Institute of Human Relations.

Menzies Lyth, I.E.P. (1992) *Containing Anxiety in Institutions, Selected essays, Volume 1*. London: Free Association Press.

Merry, T. (2002) *Learning Person-Centred Counselling*, 2nd edn. Ross-on-Wye: PCCS Books.

Milgram, S. (1974) *Obedience to Authority*. New York: Harper & Row.

Miller, E.J. and Gwynne, G.V. (1972) *A Life Apart*. London: Tavistock.

Mills, C.K. and Wooster, A.D. (1987) 'Crying in the counselling situtation', *British Journal of Guidance and Counselling*, 15: 125–30.

Mitchell, J. (2000) *Mad Men and Medusas: Reclaiming Hysteria and the Effects of Sibling Relations on the Human Condition*. Harmondsworth: Penguin.

Monckton Inquiry (1945) HMSO.

Moreno, J. L. (1934) *Who Shall Survive? A New Approach to the Problems of Human Interrelations*, Washington, DC: Nervous and Mental Diseases Publishing Co.

Mueller, E. and Brenner, J. (1977) 'The origin of social skills and interaction among playgroup toddlers', *Child Development*, 48: 854–61.

Murray, R. (1998) 'Communicating about ethical dilemmas: A medical humanities approach', in R. Bayne, P. Nicolson and I. Horton (eds) *Counselling and Communication Skills for Medical and Health Practitioners*. Oxford: Blackwell.

Myers, I.B. with Kirby, L.K. and Myers, K.D. (1998) *Introduction to Type*. OPP, 6th ed.

Myers, I. B., McCaulley, M. H., Quenk, N. L., and Hammer, A. L. (1998) *Manual: A Guide to the Development and Use of the Myers-Briggs Type Indicator*, 3rd edn. Palo Alto, CA: Consulting Psychologists Press.

Myers, I.B. with Myers, P.B. (1980) *Gifts Differing*. Palo Alto, CA: Consulting Psychologists Press.

Myers, K.D. and Kirby, L.K. (1994) *Introduction to Type Dynamics and Type Development*. Palo Alto, CA: Consulting Psychologists Press.

Newcomb, T.M. (1953) *Social Psychology: A Study of Human Interaction*. London: Routledge & Kegan Paul.

Newsom, J. T. (1999) 'Another side to care-giving: negative reactions to being helped', *Current Directions in Psychological Science*, 8: 183–7.

Nichols, K. (2003) *Psychological Care for Ill and Injured People*. Maidenhead: Open University Press.

Nicolson, P. (1994) *The Experience of Being Burgled*. Unpublished report for Frizzell Financial Services, Bournemouth, UK.

Nicolson, P. (1996) *Gender, Power and Organisation: A Psychological Perspective*. London: Routledge.

Nicolson, P. (1998) *Postnatal Depression: Psychology, Science and the Transition to Motherhood*. London: Routledge.

Nicolson, P. (2000) *Postnatal Depression: Facing the Paradox of Loss, Happiness and Motherhood*. Wiley: Chichester.

Nicolson, P. and Bayne, R. (1984/1990) *Applied Psychology for Social Workers*. London: Macmillan – now Basingstoke: Palgrave Macmillan.

Obholzer, A. and Zagier Roberts, V. (1994) *The Unconscious at Work: Individual and Organisational Stress in the Human Services*. London: Routledge.

Orbach, S. (1999) *The Impossibility of Sex*. Harmondsworth: Penguin.

Owen, J. and Cooke, J.M. (2004) 'Developing research capacity and collaboration in primary care and social care: Is there enough common ground?', *Qualitative Social Work*, 3(4).

Packman, J. (1975) *The Child's Generation*. London: Blackwell & Robertson.

Parke, R.D. *et al.* (1979) *Child Psychology: A Contemporary Viewpoint*. New York: McGraw-Hill.

Parkes, C.M. (1972) *Bereavement: Studies of Grief in Adult Life*. New York: International Universities Press.

Parkes, C.M. (1996) 'Attachment, bonding and psychiatric problems after bereavement in adult life', in C.M. Parkes, J. Stevenson-Hinde and P. Marris (eds) *Attachment Across the Life Cycle*. London: Routledge.

Parry, G. (1990) *Coping with Crises*. London: Routledge.

Parton, N. (2004) 'From Maria Colwell to Victoria Climbié: Reflections on public inquiries into child abuse a generation apart', *Child Abuse Review*, 13(2): 80–94.

Payne, M. (1982) *Working in Teams*. London: Macmillan – now Basingstoke: Palgrave Macmillan.

Pennebaker, J.W., Colder, M. and Sharp, L.K. (1990) 'Accelerating the coping process', *Journal of Personality and Social Psychology*, 58: 528–37.

Pfeiffer, E. (1977) 'Psychopathology and social pathology', in J.E. Birren and K.W. Schaie (eds) *Handbook of the Psychology of Ageing*. New York: Academic Press.

Piaget, J. (1932) *The Moral Judgement of the Child*. New York: Free Press.

Pincus, L. (1976) *Death and the Family*. London: Faber & Faber.

Provost, J.A. (1993) *Applications of the Myers-Briggs Type Indicator in Counselling: A Casebook*, 2nd edn. Gainesville, FL: Centre for Application of Psychological Type.

Quenk, N.L., Hammer, A.L. and Majors, M.S. (2001) *MBTI Step II Manual*. Palo Alto, CA: Consulting Psychologists Press.

Rainer, T. (1978) *The New Diary*. New York: St. Martin's Press.

Rainer, T. (1980) *The New Diary*. London: Angus & Robertson.

Rakos, R. (1991) *Assertive Behaviour: Theory, Research and Training*. London: Routledge.

Raphael, B. (1977) 'Preventative intervention with the recently bereaved', *Archives of General Psychology*, 34: 1450–4.

Rice, L.N. (1974) 'The evocative function of the therapist', in D. Wexler and L.N. Rice (eds) *Innovation in Client-Centred Therapy*. New York: Wiley.

Richards, M. and Light, P. (1986) *Children of Social Worlds*. Cambridge: Polity Press.

Richards, M. and Righton, P. (1972) *Social Work Education in Conflict*. London: NISW Papers.

Richman, N. (1976) 'Depression in mothers of pre-school children', *Journal of Child Psychology and Psychiatry*, 17: 25–78.

Roberts, B. (2000) *Biographical Research*. Milton Keynes: Open University Press.

Rogers, C. (1961/2002) *On Becoming a Person: A Therapists View of Psychotherapy*. London: Constable.

Rogers, C. (1975) 'Empathic: an unappreciated way of being', in C. Rogers, *A Way of Being*. Boston: Houghton Mifflin.

Rogers, C. (1987) 'Comments on the issue of equality in psychotherapy', *Journal of Humanistic Psychology*, 27: 38–40.

Rose, H. and Rose, S. (2000) *Alas Poor Darwin: Arguments against Evolutionary Psychology*. London: Jonathan Cape.

Rosenthal, T. (1993) 'To soothe the savage breast', *Behaviour Research and Therapy*, 31(5): 439–62.